To counter enemy attacks aga... Swedish Ranger Combat Swim... infiltration attacks.

Combat Frogmen

Combat Frogmen

Military diving from the nineteenth century
to the present day

Michael G. Welham

Foreword by The Right Hon Paddy Ashdown MP

Patrick Stephens Limited

First published in 1989

British Library Cataloguing in Publication Data
Welham, Michael G.
  Combat frogmen.
  1. Military operation. Underwater diving,
  to 1988
  I. Title
  359.9'84
  ISBN 1-85260-217-1

Patrick Stephens Limited is part of the Thorsons Publishing Group, Wellingborough, Northamptonshire NN8 2RQ, England.

Printed by Butler & Tanner, Frome, Somerset

Typeset by Burns & Smith, Derby

10   9   8   7   6   5   4   3   2   1

Contents

Acknowledgements

The author wishes to thank those whose assistance has been invaluable in the preparation of this book:

Jacqueline and Julie Welham – word processing
Mandy Little – agent
Bruce Quarrie – editorial work
David Gibbons
Lt.-Com. D.B. Sandiford – Officer Commanding RN Diving School
W.D. John Dadd, RN Diving School
Commandant General's Office – Royal Marines
Royal Marines Museum
Royal Marines, Poole
Royal Navy Public Relations M.o.D.
Army Public Relations M.o.D.
Royal Engineers Museum – Chatham
Ms Anna Urband – Dept of Records US Navy
Robert A. Carlisle and Russel D. Egnor – Dept of Photography US Navy
B.F. Cavalcantie – US Naval Historical Centre
US Army Special Warfare Centre
S.P.C. Dalziel & Staff – Soviet Studies Research Centre Sandhurst
Mr A. Bell
B.U.E. Sub-Sea
Cdr. H. Oswell – Submarine Products
Perry Offshore (USA)

Alan Cooper
Michael O'Mera
Mr L. Minson – Dunlop Ltd
Mrs G. Caruthers
Siebe Gorman & Co Ltd
Royal Netherlands Navy
Royal Netherlands Marine Corps
The Australian Special Air Service
The West German Navy
South African Department of Defence
Swedish Ministry of Defence
French Ministry of Defence
The Embassy of Israel
Vickers Shipbuilding & Engineering Ltd
Scicon Ltd
The Staff of Colman Road Library, Norwich
The Danish Ministry of Defence
The Imperial War Museum
C. Smagge
P. Gouldsbury
P. Croydon
P. Cooper
K. Skinner
J. Norris
M. Horeman
MGW Picture Library

Also those who have been omitted from the list by request or oversight, but who provided information or photographs.

Foreword

by the Rt. Hon. Paddy Ashdown MP

I have been lucky enough to have done a wide variety of things in my life. But one of the ones I am proudest of was to qualify as a Swimmer Canoeist and then to command a unit of Britain's Special Boat Service in the Far East.

The world of the combat swimmer is a lonely and silent one, where life constantly rests on the efficiency of your equipment, the courage of your colleague and the effectiveness of your preparation.

I know that those, like Mike Welham, with whom I served in the British SBS are the most professional colleagues I shall ever have the privilege to work with. And I am certain that the same comradeship and dedication exists amongst the combat swimmers of all nations.

Mr Welham's book provides a useful and extensive compendium of facts about this specialized world. Some will no doubt enjoy the colourful accounts of various operations. But for me the book is at its best when dealing with factual information about equipment, training and history.

Inevitably, information about combat swimmer forces of the Western nations is more readily available and reliable and it is here that Mr Welham is at his most authoritative.

For those interested in military affairs, this book will provide an indispensible source of information. For others it will provide a fascinating insight into one of the most dangerous and daring areas of warfare. For me it provides a dedication to a group of people whose skills I was proud to share and whose comradeship I was lucky enought to enjoy.

Paddy Ashdown
House of Commons
January 1989

Introduction

The role and operations of divers and covert swimmers during the Second World War are known in great detail, but in the post-war period, although the role has remained the same, the methods have changed in response to technical developments. Today, the covert swimmers' and divers' operations are shrouded in great secrecy, and even within the special forces infrastructure, they retain an air of mystery. Most people can accept the role of 'conventional' special forces, but for those who use water as a method of infiltration or of carrying out covert operations, it is a world of the unknown and unseen. The divers and swimmers involved in covert units wish to remain unknown and unseen, since the success of future operations, both in limited wars and in any major conflict, could depend upon secrecy enforced today.

With some 70 per cent of the Earth's surface consisting of water, it is not surprising that warfare both on and under this vast expanse has played an important part in all major and many minor conflicts. Most nations rely on that water for their very existence by way of trade and transport. Tankers, bulk carriers and cargo ships of many forms and sizes ply the oceans, maintaining vital trade. In times of conflict, to halt those movements could cripple a nation and force it into submission. Therefore countries must keep their sea lanes open, along with their harbours and docks.

Below the surface of these waters is a giant arena, the scene for a different type of warfare. For the most part the contenders are almost silent, and unseen: nuclear-powered submarines, capable of high speeds whilst underwater, undertaking voyages of months without surfacing. Their destructive capability, by either missiles or torpedoes, makes them a formidable force, and they, along with their counterparts, the conventional submarines, ply the trade routes seeking enemy shipping targets.

Into that silent world, often cold and cruel, with little or no visibility, and fighting not only an enemy's aggressive defences but also the tides, currents and storm-tossed seas, go the divers and swimmers. These highly trained underwater swimmers, operating in small groups, may drop by parachute, jump from hovering helicopters, launch from submerged submarines, or be carried to the target by a great variety of surface craft. They work in docks, under ships, in harbour entrances, undertaking tasks as diverse as clearing mines and constructing river crossings.

Using divers in underwater warfare is not new. Records show that Alexander the Great employed divers who used equipment enabling them to remain underwater for some considerable time. By 1203 underwater attacks on ships in warfare were considered an acceptable form of damaging the enemy. The divers employed upon such hazardous missions were provided with special helmets, to protect them from missiles thrown from the ships which they were endeavouring to attack.

It is quoted in an old ship's roll that, among the various items of weaponry supplied to ships in 1369–75 were 'Ketelhattes'. The earliest diving bells have been referred to as Kettles, so it may be assumed that 'Ketelhattes' was the terminology used for a kind of diving helmet.

In Great Britain, military diving had its real beginnings in 1837, with the invention by Augustus Siebe of his Closed Diving Dress (which we refer to today as the Standard Diving Dress). It was heavy and cumbersome on the surface, and required men to operate a pump, providing a continuous supply of air to the dress; below the surface the diver was dry and warm, and able to work for hours in shallow depths. The Royal Engineers pioneered the art of diving with this dress and undertook salvage operations, and as they gained experience, passed on the lessons learned to the Royal Navy. Diving and diving equipment changed very little throughout the ensuing years.

The First World War found a variety of uses for the diver, although, as with other unorthodox operations, the diver was viewed with a certain amount of scepticism by the conformists. The dramatic expansion in underwater operations came in the Second World War. The Italians pioneered the method of having men in rubber suits, capable of riding torpedoes into an enemy's harbour, setting a charge under a warship and sneaking out before detonation.

Siebe Gorman and Dunlop came on to the scene with equipment in the form of thin flexible suits, and an underwater breathing set which could be used from small craft, able to recirculate the oxygen so as not to give off any tell-tale bubbles which could be seen by an alert enemy defence. With the suits and underwater breathing sets, fins were developed, to fit on the divers' feet to aid propulsion, and these gave rise to the term 'frogman'.

The war years found a vast range of tasks for divers, and many specialist units were formed for a variety of jobs. The Royal Navy, Royal Marines and Royal Engineers undertook the bulk of bomb and mine disposal, salvage and construction work: Naval and Marine divers/swimmers found themselves in midget submarines. The Royal Marines Boom Patrol Detachment (RMBPD), the Army Special Boat Section and the Special Air Service all used swimmers and canoeists, as did other small specialist units. It was a period of interchange of ideas and personnel, all vying for jobs and new equipment.

After the war, when things settled down to a peacetime role, the Royal Navy used divers for bomb and mine disposal, and ships' divers to work on their warships. The Royal Marines had taken over the Commando role, and with it the assault swimmers of the Special Boat Section. The Royal Engineers continued to provide divers with engineering skills. Men of the Special Air Service undertook 'specialist training', in the form of underwater swimming for clandestine operations.

The attack diver/swimmer role of today differs little from his wartime counterpart, apart from more modern equipment and the more sophisticated defences which confront him. He still needs to gain access to his target unseen and unheard, and the method of transporting him within striking distance may be different. The definition of the word 'attack' is to act destructively and assault, and for the attack diver/swimmer this covers a multitude of operations, from limpet mine raids to bridge-building for armoured front line troops; all are assaults on the enemy.

Dramatic strides in deep saturation diving have taken place over the last few years. The expansion of the offshore oil and gas industry with its need for deep diving development has aided technology. Ships capable of setting up on one spot and remaining there for days or weeks, without anchors, but by the use of computers and dynamic positioning: remote operated vehicles, carrying underwater television cameras, able to see where man cannot in low light conditions, can undertake limited tasks using manipulators, operated by a surface control hundreds of feet above them. Depth-wise they can go where man cannot.

The titles, frogman, diver and swimmer are all used within this book, and much confusion can arise from definining the description and role of each: the word 'frogman' derives from the Second World War, and the period immediately after. Today the media still tend to use the term, but the military shun it, and in the 1980s the word is not normally found in their language.

The word 'frogman' originated from the fact that they wore black rubber suits and large rubber extensions on their feet, the latter to aid propulsion through the water: in that period, 'divers' wore the heavy Siebe Gorman Standard Diving Dress with its cumbersome brass helmet, thus creating a true demarcation between the two.

Today we concern ourselves with the two titles for underwater operatives, diver and swimmer. Both wear the same equipment, although it may be with some modifications. The Royal Navy 'diver' will attack a ship in much the same equipment as the Royal Marines 'swimmer'. The dividing line, if there is one, is that clandestine operatives use the word swimmer, as they use the water to swim on or under. Divers swim and work under the water. The diver working at depths of 1,000 feet uses similar equipment to that used at 50 feet, the difference being in technology, in so far as the breathing mixture will be vastly different, and the deep divers work from sophisticated diving bells. One thing can be defined without doubt, and that is that whichever title the men use, they all use special apparatus that enables them to breathe underwater.

This is the story of the men who, wearing different uniforms and cap badges, undertake gruelling, demanding training, where the failure rate is high, to equip themselves physically and mentally to undertake tasks in a black, cold, silent and alien environment, under the water.

Chapter 1
The origins of military diving

Men have ventured below the waves in the military context for a great number of years. It was their inventiveness, determination, sense of adventure and bravery over the years, which resulted in a transition from the heavy diving dress to the free swimming frogmen with their closed-circuit underwater swimming apparatus.

The father of diving in the British armed forces was General Sir Charles Pasley, KCB. Born on 8 September 1780, he entered the Royal Military Academy in August 1796, and was commissioned into the Royal Engineers in April 1798. He established a Survey and Civil Engineering School at Chatham in Kent, and because of his skill in engineering and explosives he was, during the year of 1837, tasked with the removal of two wrecks from the entrance of the River Thames, close to Gravesend.

Elsewhere in the country another person, of the genius-inventor mould, was putting his mind to the efforts of man working underwater. Augustus Siebe had arrived in Britain in 1816, the year following Napoleon's defeat at Waterloo, and had worked in London as an inventor. His first attempt at developing an underwater suit followed the experiments of an acquaintance who had developed an open apparatus. Siebe improved upon this and his first

The father of diving in the British armed forces, General Sir Charles Pasley KGB.

Sapper diver in standard dress of the period, the middle 1800s. One of Britain's first military divers.

system comprised a metal helmet attached by rivets to a jacket extending below the waist. Air was supplied through a hose from a pump, and surplus air escaped from the bottom of the jacket. The user could only stand, for if he leaned forward the helmet would fill up with water.

In 1837 Siebe produced his 'closed' flexible diving dress. This new apparatus was a one piece suit with shaped rubber cuffs making a watertight seal at the wrists, and a rubber collar at the neck, which was formed to meet the shape of the corselet. The helmet was locked on to the corselet by an eighth turn interlock system. The suit was completely sealed and the diver could bend over without flooding problems. With the suit, the diver wore special lace-up boots, each weighing 18 lbs, plus front and back weights which were hung over the corselet and weighed 40 lb each. On the surface a team of men helped the diver dress and enter the water. The surface team also had to hand-pump the air supplied into the helmet.

Sir Charles Pasley of the Royal Engineers was working at the same time with underwater explosives to destroy the two Thames wrecks. He had to contend with two major problems. The first was producing a reliable fuse that would work underwater; the second was the placing of the charges in the swift running river. The first problem he overcame by developing a sealed waterproof charge and a special reliable fuse. The second problem of how to place it was solved by Augustus Siebe's new diving dress.

With his team of Royal Engineers, Sir Charles began the task of removing the wrecks of the brig *Welham* and the schooner *Glenmorgan*, and by 1838 they had almost completed the job.

So successful was the combination of the Royal Engineer divers and Siebe's diving dress that Pasley was called to London, where he was given the Freedom of the City, in recognition of his exploits on the two wrecks. The developments did not go unnoticed, and he was appointed to the task of removing the wreck of the *Royal George*, as well as two other wrecks which were fouling the anchorage at Spithead. The Engineers worked for almost five years, and became very proficient in the art of diving and underwater demolition. The Royal Navy had observed the diving operations and sent men of their own to become skilled in the use of the equipment, thus forming the first combined services diving team.

Chapter 2
The Royal Marine Boom Patrol Detachment

At the outbreak of the Second World War, divers in the British armed forces were well trained in the use of the Siebe Gorman standard diving dress. Tried and tested over the years, it proved its worth, and indeed is still in production today. It was heavy and cumbersome out of the water, and still required a team of men on the surface to keep one man below: among the modernization items to the equipment was the mechanical air compressor.

The Royal Navy carried a diving team on all warships larger than a frigate, and in the case of capital ships, two or three teams. Restrictions were imposed by the bulkiness of the diver's equipment, and the lines which carried his air and telephone communications. All divers had to be familiar with hand signals on their lines, and during training the communication telephone was not used.

To work under a ship required dropping a

At the outbreak of the Second World War, divers in the British armed forces were trained in the use of the Siebe Gorman standard diving dress.

A Royal Navy standard diver enters the water to work on a submarine. The equipment was cumbersome, but it was all that was available at this period.

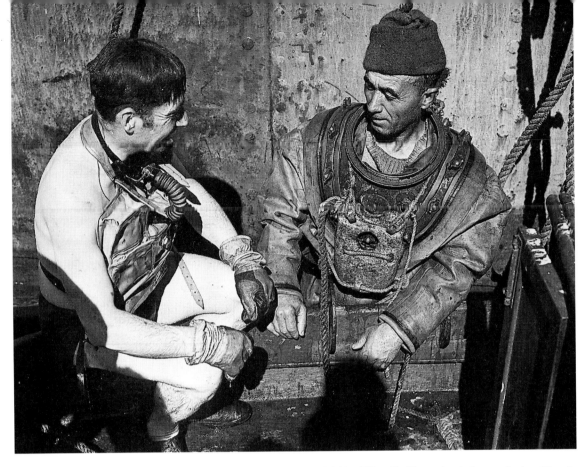

The only equipment available for underwater searches was the Standard Diver Equipment, the DSEA. This was cumbersome for searching the bottom of a ship.

rope over the bows, the ends being held by men who would then walk astern, either side, pulling the rope along. When in place, the rope would be pulled up tight, so that it ran from one side of the ship, under the hull and up the other side. The diver was dressed whilst sitting either in a small ship's boat, or on a platform which was lowered from the ship's deck into the water. The rope was his shot rope, which he held on to, to guide and support him. If he needed to go for'ard or astern, the deck crews dragged their rope ends in the direction indicated. This laborious, time-consuming job of working on or inspecting the bottom of ships was accepted at this period, for no other equipment was available. The divers themselves were trained and familiar with the apparatus, and once skilled could perform many useful tasks.

The first round in a new form of underwater warfare went to the Axis powers, as early as 1941. The Italians had formed the Tenth Light Flotilla, the Gamma Group, a unit whose leaders had speculated on the use of men riding underwater machines, entering enemy harbours to attack ships at anchor. The first attack came to Gibraltar, which abounded in merchant vessels en route for the war fronts in North Africa, where they deposited fuel and stores for use by Allied warships and aircraft. Three controllable torpedoes, each ridden by two men, entered the harbour, where targets were selected and the torpedoes then submerged for the final attack. Charges were placed under three British ships, two tankers and one cargo vessel, the detonations being delayed to allow the men to make good their escape. They used a form of breathing apparatus that was light in weight, self-contained, and closed circuit so as not to give off any tell-tale exhaust bubbles. The explosions were not spectacular, and people in the area heard only a loud 'thump'. The effect, on the other hand, was devastating, and for the authorities, unnerving.

Three ships had been destroyed by unseen

forces. Surveys of the sunken wrecks using the British standard diving dress, found the remains of an underwater torpedo-shaped craft, the like of which had not been seen before, and some sets of a new and unfamiliar breathing apparatus. Both items were unknown to the Allies. The Italians made their way home to a jubilant reception, for their success was the start of a damaging new type of warfare.

The success of the underwater attacks by the Italians was the culmination of five years' work. Sub-Lieutenants T. Tesei and E. Toschi of the Italian Navy had submitted plans for a human torpedo concept in 1935. Worthy of note is the fact that the firm of Siebe Gorman had developed a closed circuit underwater breathing system, called the Amphibian Mark 1, and established a factory in Italy for its production during the 1930s after the British Admiralty had rejected all advances by the company, on the grounds that the standard equipment was safer, and the possibility of using free-swimming divers as combat troops was unthinkable. The Italians, on the other hand, had the foresight to utilize the equipment and develop a craft, thus forming the first underwater special force, leaving the Allies totally unaware of such developments.

The Italian 'human torpedo' men had approached the outer perimeter of the harbour by night, to submerge at the boom defences and either cut holes through the steel mesh, or lift the net up and slide underneath, if depth permitted. They then rose just enough to allow their heads to emerge from the water. At the last moment they submerged and, using a compass bearing, moved under the target ship. The craft was then raised to come up under the ship, where clamps were fitted to the bilge keel on either side. The warhead was attached to a line running between the two clamps and detached from the craft, to hang below the hull, its delayed fuse allowing time for the crews to make good their escape.

The Admiralty reacted to the attack by asking Gibraltar command to provide an adequate counter offensive. That was easier said than done, for the only diving equipment available

Above A member of the Underwater Working Party searching the underside of a ship using Davis Submerged Escape Apparatus (DSEA).

Below Member of the UWP removes a device from the underside of a ship. He wears only swimming trunks and plimsolls and uses the DSEA. Rubber suits and fins were things of the future.

was the standard diving dress, and to use that to search all the ships passing through the harbour at that period would have been impossible.

An Underwater Working Party was formed comprising Lieutenant Bill Bailey and Leading Seaman Bell. They were tasked with the job of searching all ships entering the harbour, and if anything was found, rendering it safe. Apart from the heavy diving dress, the Davis Submerged Escape Apparatus (DSEA) was available, which had been designed by the Siebe Gorman Company to allow submariners to escape from damaged and submerged boats. The set was very basic and consisted of a flexible bag, which rested on the wearer's chest, a canister which contained a carbon dioxide absorbent, a rubber hose and mouthpiece, and a small bottle of oxygen. The wearer first opened the bottle of oxygen to fill the flexible bag; then, when he breathed in, oxygen would pass through the absorbent up the hose and into the man's lungs. When he expired the breath, it returned back down the hose, through the absorbent and into the bag, the carbon dioxide having been removed. He could continue to breathe in this way from some time.

Bailey and Bell procured some of these sets, and trained themselves in their use. Dressed in swimming costumes, they would climb down a ladder into the water, and continue breathing. A small pair of goggles kept their eyes clear of the salt water, as they moved about and ascertained the limitations of the apparatus.

On the surface they learned how to charge the oxygen bottles. Nobody knew how to maintain the equipment, so they did not bother. Training was done in a single day, the final phase being to ride a launch out to a ship, then jump into the water and using breaststroke movement, make their way to the bilge keel of the ship. They were free to move in any direction, and did so, looking for anything that was not meant to be there. The task completed, new recruits were duly made members of the Underwater Working Party.

Bailey had one claim to a first: whilst inspecting the underside of a ship he observed a

Training was undertaken in a single day and began with familiarity on the surface with the DSEA.

shape moving through the water. He thought it was a fish but soon saw that it was another frogman. Certain that it was not a friendly one, he drew his knife and attacked. The knife penetrated the frogman's rubber suit, but before Bailey could do more damage, the enemy swam away, aided by the flippers which British frogmen lacked at this time.

Lionel Philip Kenneth Crabb was a member of the RNVR at the outbreak of the Second World War, and was one of the most unusual men to become a naval diver. At the age of 32, he was totally opposed to any form of exercise and only just able to swim three lengths of a swimming pool. Once in the Navy he sought the unusual, and became trained in the art of bomb and mine disposal. His first post was to Gibraltar

Training involved putting goggles in place, mouthpiece between teeth, and climbing down the ladder.

Lt. Lionel Philip Kenneth Crabb RNVR.

in 1942 where, apart from the normal EOD (Explosive Ordnance Disposal) duties, he had to dispose of mines recovered by divers.

He met the diving team, which then consisted of only Bailey and Bell, and enquired as to their task. He was informed that they had to inspect the hulls of both warships and merchantmen, at anchor in the harbour. The team had equipment of a very basic nature, and no special underwater suits. They searched the hulls of the ships, day or night, rain or shine, dressed in overalls and plimsolls, and using underwater breathing apparatus that was designed for escaping from stricken submarines.

As was his nature, Crabb decided that since he was the principal mine disposal officer, he ought to join these men in their underwater task.

So he undertook his diving training in Gibraltar harbour. Dressed in a pair of overalls and gym shoes, he was introduced to the Davis Submerged Escape Aparatus. Donning the set, he climbed down the ladder to the water's surface. Then, putting a pair of goggles in place and the mouthpiece between his teeth, he continued down the ladder. Below the surface he gained confidence in the ability both to breathe and to move about underwater. Returning to the surface, he found his introduction was short lived, as the alarm was raised, indicating that a ship needed inspection. Crabb required no bidding, and joined the other two divers on the job. He dived under his first ship, beginning an underwater career that was to make him a legend in military diving.

As the demand for their services grew, the Underwater Working Party needed to recruit, and so posted a notice for volunteers. The best men, on both ships and shore establishments, were refused permission to join by their respective COs, and the initial group (some of whom looked upon this underwater work as a cushy number) was rejected, but enough of good material was accepted and spirited away. One useful addition for the hard-working party was a senior rating who had done a maintenance course on Davis Submarine Escape Apparatus. It was he who discovered that the CO_2 absorbent had to be changed after every dive. In ignorance, the Underwater Party had used the same absorbent for a week at a time, and had been remarkably fortunate not to have suffered from CO_2 poisoning.

These men of the Underwater Working Party (now under the command of Crabb) worked around the clock searching the tankers, cargo ships and liberty ships, full of men, for explosive charges. It was a job which could not stop, for even though they worked hard, the Italians were still able to penetrate the harbour and inflict damage, although it became harder, and more costly for them. The Underwater Working Party set up underwater counter-attack defences, and if anybody thought they saw anything in the water, explosive charges were dropped in the area by very keen crews, in the patrol boats.

In December 1941 the Italians moved their scene of operations to Alexandria where, for some reason, no underwater working party for the inspection of ships at harbour had been established. It appears that the reality of underwater attack had not been fully accepted. The main Italian targets were the battleships *Queen Elizabeth* and *Valiant*. Six men and their three small craft were carried within range by submarine, where they were launched and headed for the harbour. Slipping in unseen, two of the

The Italians were able to penetrate Gibraltar harbour and inflict serious damage using chariots and operating from a sunken ship in Spanish waters.

craft made for the two battleships while the other made for a tanker; although the crews were captured, two of them by the *Valiant*, the Royal Navy did not know if their task had been successful until the charges detonated, crippling the three ships.

* * *

Whilst the specialist underwater teams began to develop new equipment and train in the 'frogman' underwater swimming apparatus, the results of the Italian underwater attacks left Alexandria harbour blocked, with sunken ships. These wrecks had to be removed and it fell to the Navy and Marine divers to do the job, using the conventional standard diving dress. The ships lay on the bottom, many on their sides, and had to be cut and levelled by the use of explosive charges.

By nature of the environment in which they work, divers have to be inventive, and a new method of placing a cutting charge was developed. The divers would go down to the wrecked ship and push a wooden pole underneath. Atached to one end would be a thin rope, which led up to the dive boat on the surface. The pole, which protruded out of the other side, was pulled through and, being wood, floated to the surface. The crew on the surface collected the pole and pulled the rope, which now had two ends on the surface and passed under the wreck. To one end of the rope a canvas hose, already filled with explosive, was tied and pulled down under the wreck. A series of such hoses would be run at intervals along the wreck and then connected by an electric detonation wire, which terminated on the surface. The divers would be recovered from the water, and the boats cleared of the area, then the charges were detonated. This process would be repeated until the wrecks were levelled low enough as to no longer block the harbour.

Harbours on the East Coast of Britain were the home of various smaller military craft. At Great Yarmouth in East Anglia, motor torpedo boats and similar types of operational craft were stationed. The propellers of these craft were very susceptible to damage and many were found to have only three of the four blades left, or ropes, wires and parachute lines fouling them. On return from each operation, therefore, their skippers would request an underwater examination. Large flat-bed lorries, commandeered for the duration by the War Office, carried all the diving equipment, including a long ladder. The divers would arrive, display the red flag used for 'divers down' (of which nobody took the slightest notice) and then don the Standard diving equipment. The ladder would be placed on the bottom, resting against the jetty wall, and in a position to enable the diver to stand on it and work on the vessel's propeller. The port of Great Yarmouth is long and narrow, and is susceptible to strong tides, which creates a 'no visibility' situation. This was combined with the coming and going of craft which created a wash, causing movement of the vessel being worked on, and making the task difficult.

The harbour was vulnerable to attack from enemy E-boats, and so a pattern of 21 mines was laid around the entrance, controlled by one central observation post. If the enemy had raided, the observers would have waited and when the craft were within the pattern, the mines would have been detonated, placing those craft in the confines of an extremely effective trap.

* * *

Prior to the attack on the capital ships in Alexandria harbour, Captain H.G. 'Blondie' Hasler, Royal Marines, who was serving with the Mobile Naval Base Defence Organization, had put together a proposal and submitted it to the appropriate authorities, which would involve the use of canoes to carry men dressed in flexible rubber diving suits into enemy harbours, who would then place mines on the unsuspecting enemy ships. The Admiralty rejected his proposal. Hasler was not deterred, like others, such as David Stirling and Orde Wingate, whose unorthodox ideas had faced rejection, but persevered until the concept found the right desk. Hasler took his papers and rewrote them, adding that such underwater trained swimmers would be able to undertake beach reconnaissance and to mark and destroy underwater obstacles, especially in probable landing areas. He presented the revised proposals, and waited for some response. None came. The papers moved from desk to desk, department to department. Ironically, it was the Italians who made the decision, in a roundabout way. After their successful attack on the two battleships, demands came from the highest quarter of the Royal Navy for explanations as to why the raids had been so successful, what the Navy was doing to counter them, and even more important, why the British did not have the capability to carry out such raids in return.

The faceless ones who had passed Hasler's papers around hastily found them, and presented them for approval: they were accepted and Hasler was called to develop a unit which could carry out the raids he had described. The unit would consist of Royal Marines, as they had links with the sea, and most had one other very useful commodity, being commando-trained. Every man was to be a volunteer, and it was agreed that Hasler should command the unit. The unit was trained for the purpose of undertaking raids using small craft and developing a new form of underwater swimming.

Formed in Portsmouth during June 1942, the new unit bore the name of Royal Marine Boom Patrol Detachment, a name created to give the impression that it would patrol and maintain the defence booms at the entrance to Portsmouth harbour. Secrecy was to be the byword for the unit.

The RMBPD procured the only underwater diving dress available, the Sladden suit, again developed for submariners when escaping from their submerged submarines, and the Davis Submarine Escape Apparatus. The suit was unsuitable for what Hasler had in mind, for

RMBPD's close-fitting rubber suit which enabled the wearer to move freely for use in canoes and other small craft.

it was too loose fitting, being made of thin silk and rubber, even though it covered the body (sealing at the wrists), and incorporated a hood with a small fixed glass face piece, which could if required be lifted up. Roughly-made canvas boots were worn, allowing the wearer to walk or crawl around the bottom. A large breathing bag was attached to the chest and was connected to the hood by a gas mask breathing hose pipe. Two large oxygen bottles were carried on the back, these in fact being products of Germany! They were made of an aluminium alloy which was highly suitable for underwater use, but this being unobtainable in wartime Britain, they were removed from shot-down German aircraft.

RMBPD submitted instead a design for a thin, flexible, close-fitting suit, which would enable the wearer to move freely, climbing in and out of canoes and other small craft, as well as being easily fitted and keeping the wearer dry.

The Admiralty Diving Committee reviewed RMBPD's request and was sceptical, due to concern over how the diver would keep warm. However Hasler's needs were serious, if he was to do the job he had been delegated, and he was eventually introduced to the Dunlop Rubber Company, where the problem was presented. Dunlop had nothing to do with the manufacture of diving suits, but were involved with balloons and flying suits. The end result was a close-fitting suit of rubberized stockinet, which had a neck flexible enough to allow a man to enter through. Rubber cuffs completed the seal at the wrists, and so kept the wearer dry. A separate hood was developed to enable the wearer to use underwater breathing apparatus or not, as required. The divers solved the problem of keeping warm by wearing combinations and a thick woollen under suit.

The bad points of the Davis Submarine Escape Apparatus had also been discussed and ideas of improvement submitted. A new and much improved underwater breathing set was therefore produced, which was more comfortable, consisting of a pair of rubberized breathing bags, mounted on a rubber jacket. The two oxygen bottles were fitted on the front, under the

bags. The wearer fitted the set over his head, so that it rested on his shoulders. The principle of the new set was the same as that of the DSEA and had the single hose, pushing and pulling the oxygen through a canister of carbon dioxide absorbent. It was again closed circuit, and gave off no tell-tale exhaust bubbles which would betray men swimming underwater, to an alert enemy defence.

RMBPD gained an addition to its ranks in the form of Lieutenant-Commander Bruce Wright, a Royal Canadian Naval Officer. He had given much thought to the use of swimmers to gain access to enemy harbours and attack their ships, and introduced two new invaluable items, to aid them. He knew that the Abalone divers in California used rubber extensions on their feet and a rubber mask that fitted over the face with a single glass plate in the front. He had a mask with him but the flippers, which were in his main baggage *en route* to Britain by sea, were lost when the ship was sunk. Further face masks were made, using the original as a model, while fins were produced from drawings. The RMBPD was elated, for these new items would complete the equipment for an underwater swimmer. Hasler's operatives, skilled in the use of canoes and paddling rubber inflatable boats, trained with the underwater equipment to complete the final part of their clandestine raiding programme, using Eastney swimming baths (when closed to others) and Horsea Lake for training.

* * *

Axis vessels were running the blockade from Bordeaux, which was to provide the target for RMBPD's first canoe raid. Hasler was to lead men from the unit on Operation 'Frankton', an attack on the ships loading in the port, which lies some 100 km up the River Gironde. Five canoes were launched from a submarine on the night of 7 December 1942, close to the river's entrance; then, paddling by night and hiding by day, the men made the journey up the river.

The full exploits of the raid are well

Above RMBPD swimmer canoeists dressed in their new rubber suits, utilizing canoes for their new operational role.

Below RMBPD build stamina on arduous rubber boat paddling exercises.

Above RMBPD team wearing underwater breathing apparatus paddling rubber boat during a training exercise in Eastney swimming baths.

Below Combat frogmen training on various operational underwater tasks in Eastney swimming pool.

A canoeist passes a limpet mine to a frogman.

documented, and are depicted in the film *Cockleshell Heroes*. Of those who reached the docks to find the enemy ships and undertake the final attack, the frogmen sitting in the front seats of the canoes had to carefully extricate themselves and gain access to the water. The canoeists remained in the boat, keeping the craft in the shadows, and passed the primed limpet mines to the frogmen. As they worked around the ships, enemy guards patrolled above them and on harbour launches. Each frogman, holding his mine, would submerge alongside a ship's hull, to find the delicate area near the engine room, then clamp the mine on to the steel hull plates. He would then surface carefully, and move to the next location.

Of the ten men who left on the raid, only two were to return, Hasler and Marine Bill Sparks, and that was after using the overland escape route. The other eight were shot, following Hitler's directive that all 'special forces' troops were to be categorized as saboteurs and spies, and dealt with as such. Apart from the loss of the men, the raid was a success, and proved that both the canoe and frogman could be used in clandestine operations.

* * *

Experiments in the use of underwater craft were carried out during this period.

Whilst the RMBPD carried out the raids for which it was raised, it also became involved in experiments. One involved a small motor boat, designated the Boom Defence Boat, which was adapted to fit into a Lancaster's bomb bay. Over the target area, the diver would climb into the craft, wearing underwater breathing apparatus and a personal parachute. At five thousand feet, the craft would be launched into mid air. Three parachutes would then deploy to lower the craft to the sea below, disengaging themselves once the craft was afloat. Although

the diver wore a personal parachute it was very much doubted if he would ever be able to extricate himself from the craft to use it. During 1944, drops with men on board were successfully made, but if the system was ever used on a raid, there are no detailed records.

A more successful experiment was undertaken with a motorized submersible canoe, known to those involved with it as the 'sleeping beauty'. It was constructed of mild steel plate and aluminium, almost 3.9 m (13 ft) long and with a beam of slightly more than 60 cm (2 ft). It was driven by a $\frac{1}{2}$ hp electric motor, drawing its power from four six-volt car batteries, and could attain a speed of some 4.5 knots on the surface, and 3.5 knots when submerged. Its range at full

power was about twelve miles, and up to forty miles at cruising speed. It could be paddled or sailed, and had a mast and sail made from parachute silk included as additional equipment.

One man operated the craft, wearing the new underwater swim suit and breathing apparatus. A single stick controlled the direction, and by flooding the buoyancy tanks it could be

Left Experiments with motorized canoes began in the swimming pool.

Below left The motorized canoe was designed to carry a limpeter to the side of a ship.

dived to an operational depth of up to 12 m (40 ft). It was remarkably stable and easy to operate. Carrying one anti-capital ship charge, or a number of limpet mines, all of which were suitable for handling underwater by the operator, it made a versatile attack platform. Because of its size the risk of detection was less than with an ordinary canoe, its low profile and lack of paddle movement combining with its submerged final approach. As far as is known, it was never used operationally, but one thing the experiments do show is the dedication of the underwater swimmers to develop methods of attack.

Chapter 3
Human torpedoes and midget submarines ·

It was 1942 when the Admiralty ordered the formation of a Human Torpedo Unit. Using the captured remains of Italian Human Torpedoes, Britain set about the task of developing similar craft. Under Commander Fell, RN, the new unit called for 'special duties' volunteers. Selections were made, and the volunteers were sent to Portsmouth to begin their training, first in the use of underwater diving equipment and then in the operation of the new 'torpedoes'. Physical training strengthened the men, who were also introduced to the water, using the Sladden suit. To produce a team spirit the officers would assist the other ranks to dress, and the men would then submerge into the water to gain experience and confidence in their equipment. The roles would then be reversed, and the other ranks would help dress the officers. The physical training and diving combined to produce the nucleus of Britain's first Human Torpedo teams, the 'Charioteers'. They did not have a torpedo to train on, as these were still in the production stage, but a mock up was produced, to give the training more authenticity.

With completion of diving training and the delivery of the first production models, the unit moved to Scotland. In Loch Corrie the men were introduced to the new craft, called by the

The Charioteers' dress, with a flip-up face plate to enable the operator to see and breathe when on the surface.

British 'Jeeps', or 'Chariots'. They were cylindrical, with a rudder, hydroplanes and propeller at the tapered tail. The fore end held the explosive warhead, and the design allowed the craft to run underwater without it. Two seats were fitted which allowed the crew to sit astride the torpedo (future developments would allow the crew to sit inside a cockpit, thus streamlining the shape). The front seat had the diving controls, luminous depth and pressure gauges, and the vital compass. Inside the body were the main battery, electric propulsion motor, air tanks and ballast pump. The craft had an operational speed of two to three knots. As with swimmers, compass bearings were taken as line of sight and any magnetic interference caused by mines or clamps remained constant.

A team consisted of a pair; 'number one', who sat in the forward position and controlled the craft, and 'number two', who sat in the aft position and undertook the task of fixing the charge to the bottom of an enemy ship. The pairs began their training on the torpedoes during daylight, and on the surface. Progressively

Britain designed and developed the underwater 'Chariot'; this example is without the explosive warhead at the nose.

Above Charioteers were introduced to the underwater equipment in training tanks.

Above right The Charioteers sat astride the vehicle.

Right The Chariot on the surface made a small target for operations in enemy waters.

they would submerge until only their heads were out of the water, and then they would go completely below the surface.

Once under the water, number one controlled the ballast, and guided the craft by using the compass. As they became confident, the submerged 'runs' became longer, and training involved avoiding detection by a keen surface group who searched for the 'charioteers' in surface vessels. Once they could handle the craft efficiently and guide them unseen to a target, they were introduced to the 'defences', in the form of anti-torpedo and submarine nets. These would

require the 'number two' to dismount, and use heavy cutters to make a hole large enough for the craft to pass through. Although light did not penetrate very far down, it gave enough illumination for the charioteers to make out shapes in the gloom. Now the skills they had learnt in daylight had to be re-enacted at night, for clandestine underwater attacks were done in the hours of darkness. The charioteers had to penetrate the nets, then proceed to the target. They would surface enough to allow their heads clear of the water, to gain a compass fix, then submerge and run underwater on the bearing. The surface party looked for them, searching with torches. The charioteers became more and more efficient. If they were found at this stage, only a torch beam shone on them; inside enemy lines, however, machine-guns and depth charges would be trained on them.

The British method of chariot attack differed from that of the Italians, in that the British would manoeuvre their craft alongside the enemy ship, and use powerful magnets to hold them in place. By moving the magnets down, they were able to guide the torpedo into position, where the warhead was secured to the magnets and disengaged from the craft, which was then able to move away. By contrast the Italians drove their torpedoes under the ship, then released ballast until they came to the ship's bottom, where they would secure clamps to the ship's bilge keel on either side. A line ran between the two clamps and it was to this that the warhead was secured to be left hanging below the hull, primed to detonate after the torpedo had left the area.

In June 1942 the Special Operations Executive, under whose wing the charioteers lived, were approached by the Navy and asked to cooperate in a plan to attack the German battleship *Tirpitz*, a very great menace to Allied merchant ships, whilst she lay at Trondheim fjord in Norway. The plan was formulated and agreed. A motor fishing vessel, the *Arthur*, was to be used as the support craft, to carry two chariots and crews across the North Sea to Norway. The chariots were then to be launched and towed through the

The British method of Chariot attack differed from that of the Italians, in that the British would manoeuvre their craft alongside the enemy ship and use powerful magnets to hold them in place.

German controls to an area where the crews could board their craft and undertake the attack. Papers were forged to allow the *Arthur* to continue as if about lawful business. Doubts about the *Tirpitz's* whereabouts arose, and it could not be confirmed that she was at Trondheim fjord, indeed intelligence reports indicated that the battleship was at Bogen fjord.

It was at the beginning of October when the order to attack was given. The *Tirpitz* was at Bogen fjord and had now sailed south. Aboard the *Arthur*, Sub-Lieutenant Brewster RNVR, Sergeant Craig, RE, Able Seaman Brown and Able Seaman Evans were the crews for the two chariots. The vessel encountered very rough weather in the North Sea, which delayed them. Then at the pre-arranged location the chariots were unlashed and made ready for the water, but the battery charging motor broke down. Sub-Lieutenant Brewster decided that enough power remained in the batteries to cover the required distance. The chariots were now being

towed behind the *Arthur*, which in late evening developed engine trouble, which meant the engine had to be stripped down. The crew was unperturbed, the repairs were done and the passage continued.

They passed the scrutiny of a German patrol boat and continued towards their target. But the weather began to worsen, causing the *Arthur* to rise and fall in the increasing waves, putting a great deal of strain on the towing wires. They steamed to a place of shelter where Evans was able to dive and examine the chariots. He followed the towing wires down to the shackles, but there were no chariots. Ironically they were within striking distance of the enemy target, the prized German battleship *Tirpitz*.

* * *

In 1942, alongside the development of the 'human torpedo' came the 'X' craft, a midget submarine. The charioteers rode outside their craft and were subjected to hours in the bitterly cold water, although they wore protective waterproof suits and insulated under-garments. The new development meant that an attack could be made in the dry, the craft being able to operate without exposing the crew to the elements.

Midget submarines were 14.4 metres (48 feet) long and had a maximum diameter of some 1.68 metres (5 ft 6 in). This meant the four men in the crew were unable to stand up straight, unless they were on the small side. The boat was divided into four compartments. The forward one contained the battery which supplied power for the ballast pumps and the auxiliary machinery; it also powered the craft when it was submerged, and it was in this compartment that the divers' equipment was stored.

The second section was called the 'wet and dry' compartment. It was an escape chamber based on those designed and fitted in the latest submarines. Although quite small, a man in diving dress could enter. The door of the compartment was sealed closed, and the diver opened a valve allowing water to enter. Once full of water, the outer hatch was opened and the diver could go outside. On re-entering the submarine, the diver would seal the outside door, then blow out the water until the compartment was dry. The inside door could then be opened, and the diver would be back inside the submarine. The use of this compartment did not alter the trim of the boat, nor did it allow water into the remainder of the compartments.

The third compartment was the main one and housed all of the controls for operating the submarine. Dozens of levers, wheels and gauges were crammed into the restricted space. The two periscopes were housed in this area, one giving a general wide field of view, the other narrow

angled for attack. Also set in this over-crowded area were the air purifiers and cooking equipment, where the most basic of food and drinks could be made. The fourth and final compartment was the home of the gyro compass, the high pressure compressor and a further mass of pipes, gauges, levers and valves.

These small craft could remain submerged for 36 hours on battery power, and when cruising the crew operated in two shifts, two men at the controls and two men resting, changing round every four hours. On the run-in for attack, all four men would man their stations, one of them dressed in the diving equipment.

The main defences encountered by these craft were the anti-submarine and torpedo nets, guarding harbour entrances. The submarine would move forward until stopped by the net.

The 'Stickleback' *X51*, an 'X' craft midget sub leaving harbour on the surface.

The diver would prepare to enter the water, then by means of the wet and dry compartment exit the craft. Often these manoeuvres were carried out at night, and in the blackness he would move to the bow of the boat. Using heavy wire croppers he would begin the job of cutting the net, making a gap large enough for the boat to pass through. When he had made the hole, he would signal to the crew inside by a series of predetermined knocks on the hull, for the boat to ease ahead. The diver would check the clearance of the boat, ensuring that it did not foul itself. Once through the boat would stop, and the diver would re-enter it.

A harbour with some important ships at anchor may have had more than one net which would have to be penetrated, some of which could be breached by going underneath. Even when the outer defences were passed, the inner areas were patrolled by surface craft, aided by asdic and radar. The major ships were almost certainly themselves surrounded by protective nets. When the submarine reached its target it could either drop a large explosive charge underneath it, or the diver could go out again and place limpet mines on its underside, all of which, obviously, would be timed to detonate after the submarine had left the target area. The chances of the submarine finding the holes in the nets on the way out would be very small, and so the diver might well have to leave the boat yet again to cut new holes.

After the unsuccessful raid by the 'human torpedoes' on the *Tirpitz*, the 'X' craft were presented with the target. The German vessel lay in the isolated fjord of Kaafjord in northern Norway. To reach the anchorage required the penetration of a minefield and a passage of fifty miles up the fjord. The journey was fraught with danger from shore defences and patrol craft. As the six midget submarines, X5–X10, entered the anchorage, they had to penetrate the anti-submarine and torpedo nets. One of the submarines had a compass failure and ran aground on an uncharted sand bank. It was spotted by an alert sentry and was subjected to a fierce counter-attack by the enemy, using depth charges. The other five craft pressed home the attack, where charges were dropped below the ship. The submarines were scuttled as the crews escaped and were captured, and although the *Tirpitz* was not sunk, she suffered enough damage to keep her out of the war for some time. It also proved that the fjords of Norway were no longer safe for enemy ships from Allied underwater attackers.

It was not long before the Germans became wise to the threat and damage caused by the underwater attacks. They strengthened their defences by guards onshore and patrol craft. Movable wooden platforms were built, which would be towed into place once a ship was moored, thus allowing the guards to walk round, near the water's surface. They were armed with sub-machine-guns, and underwater anti-personnel charges. The attack divers soon overcame the new defences and would move into the harbour and wait submerged for ships to berth. Once the vessel stopped moving and was secure, the attack divers would move in and place their charges, to depart the target before the wooden platforms and guards were in place.

The decision to proceed with 'human torpedoes', midget submarines and free-swimming frogmen in early 1942 posed a number of problems, apart from the need to design machines, suits and underwater breathing apparatus. One of these was the use of oxygen at various depths. To address the situation the Admiralty Diving Committee under the chairmanship of Rear Admiral R.B. Drake CB, DSO, established the Admiralty Experimental Diving Unit and based it at the Siebe Gorman works at Tolworth in Surrey.

The facilities available to the team included three cylindrical tanks, one 12 ft deep and 12 ft in diameter, one 25 ft deep and 6 ft in diameter and the third, was 12 ft deep and 6 ft in diameter. The fourth chamber, which became infamous to all those concerned, was the 'pot'.

A diver experiments using underwater breathing apparatus in the 'Pot'.

This chamber had a small opening in the top, and inside contained 8 ft of water, the upper 4 ft being dry. This was the place where divers would be subjected to different water depth pressures, up to a maximum of 150 ft.

The unit which arrived at Tolworth comprised sixteen experimental divers, with diving officers, instructors, medical staff and other relevant personnel required to run the unit and carry out the experiments. Two of the principal senior staff were the medical officers, Surgeon Lieutenant-Commanders K.W. Donald, DSC, MD, RN, and W.M. Davidson, MB, BCh, RN, and the whole of the operation came under the direct control of the Superintendent of Diving.

The volunteer divers, who had answered the call for 'hazardous duties volunteers', found themselves subjected to medicals and interviews,

and being selected for the job, before they knew what was required of them. The object of the experiments was to determine the safe working depths of oxygen when breathed underwater, as well as individual tolerances. Professor J.S. Haldane was heavily involved and controlled many of the experimental 'dives'. For the individuals undertaking the experiment, it was an unnerving experience.

Each diver was lowered, dressed in closed circuit underwater breathing apparatus, into the water in the 'pot', while an attendant entered the top section and controlled the life line. Then the steel door was closed, two heavy and strong steel backing plates were set into place and the door bolted shut. Finally a hammer was used on a spanner to make sure the bolts were secure. The sound of the noise would echo around the small steel area, indicating that the diver was firmly locked in and could not be released very quickly in the event of trouble. The chamber was then pressurized to equal a water depth of 50 ft, the diver remaining under the water breathing oxy-

When the diver's lips began to tingle and twitch, he would move them around the mouthpiece until the sensation disappeared.

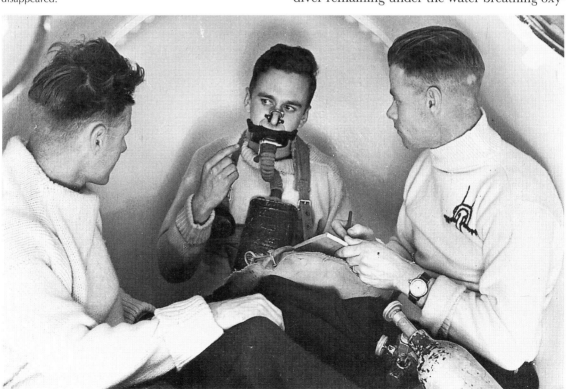

gen. When his lips began to tingle and twitch, he would move them around the mouthpiece until the sensation disappeared. He would remain in the chamber for a set period, or until he passed out. The attendant would assist until the hatch could be opened and the diver taken out to recover. The divers invented a demon whom they called 'Oxygen Pete' who would creep up and take them over, so they competed to see who could avoid 'Pete' the longest.

More than one thousand such dives were undertaken, often resulting in the divers suffering convulsions and unconsciousness. Their courage was rewarded by the additional payment of five shillings per day!

Chapter 4

Combined Operations Pilotage Parties and 'P' Parties

In 1944 the specialist units of trained underwater swimmers were aware of the coming invasion of Europe, and that the Germans were preparing heavy defences along the French coastline, not only on land but in the sea. Aerial reconnaissance had observed strange objects in the sea along the coastline. If a landing was to be made in the magnitude that a full-scale assault into Europe would require, then the obstructions would have to be removed.

Until this time the underwater swimming attacks had been conducted by small groups of highly-trained men; now the demand was for sufficient divers to clear the landing beaches and remove mines and bombs from the harbours and ports as they were liberated. Apart from the manpower shortage, there was the need for more equipment, and each unit demanded different apparatus for the tasks that it would be called upon to undertake. Experiments had shown that the oxygen closed circuit sets were safe in water up to 10 m (33 ft), so for those needing to have a deeper free swimming capability, an oxygen and nitrogen mixture was required.

Combined Operations Pilotage Parties was formed in 1942 by Commander Nigel Clogtoun-Willmott with the express purpose of beach reconnaissance. After a very successful survey prior to the Allied landings on Sicily, the unit was called upon to survey the landing beaches in Normandy. The first operation in January 1944

took the swimmers into the Gold and Juno beaches where, under the noses of the enemy, they undertook full beach surveys, collecting sand and soil samples and gathering data on the obstacles, which consisted of Element 'C' (steel girder construction), 'pyramids' and 'hedge-hogs', all of which were festooned with explosives.

The second recce was to be of the Americans' Omaha and Utah beaches, and for this operation the divers used a converted 'X' craft, which had had some of the demolition equipment removed to allow additional navigation equipment to be added. Swimmers went ashore and gathered the valuable samples, which determined the make-up of each beach and thus its suitability to accommodate tanks and trucks; again the beaches were found to be well-defended by underwater obstructions.

From the information gained by these reconnaissances, mock-ups of the obstructions were made, and experiments conducted to determine the best way of destroying them. Frogmen of the 'P' parties, Landing Craft Obstruction Clearance Parties, 'X' craft crews, two-man torpedo charioteers, limpeteers, the Boom Patrol Detachment and the Combined Operations Pilotage Parties, trained and prepared for the operation, upon whose success would depend that of the initial landing.

Before the first signs of dawn on 6 June 1944, the surf broke heavily on the Normandy beaches. For the occupying forces in their concrete bunkers, it was just another day. To the observer gazing out to sea, only the dark gloom of night turning to day was evident. Below the concrete fortresses lay miles of barbed wire, mines, booby traps, tank traps, in fact anything that could obstruct a frontal assault. Had those watchers realized what waited in the darkness, they would not have been relaxed. Waiting offshore were 'X' craft, rigged with coloured lights, and ready to act as markers to guide the landing craft into the safe lanes. Those midget submarines had been there for 48 hours.

The first men ashore on that memorable day were frogmen of the Landing Craft Obstruction Clearance Unit, who numbered some 120 men. They were taken during the hours of darkness by landing craft as close to the Gold and Juno beaches as possible, where they prepared their breathing apparatus and preshaped explosive charges. They knew that they would be subjected to pressure waves from explosions, which travel long distances underwater, and could be killed. Specially-designed jackets known as 'Kapok jackets' were therefore worn under their rubber suits. They were so successful that frogmen close to an explosion survived blasts that killed unprotected troops in the water a considerable distance away, and it is without doubt these jackets, with their ability to absorb the shock waves, that saved many of those swimmers.

Most of those men, preparing for the biggest strike frogmen would make against the enemy, were 'hostilities only' men. They came from quite ordinary backgrounds of civilian employment: bank clerks, carpenters, engineers, students and a cotton salesmen provided an example of the mixed bag. They had all volunteered for 'special duties', not really knowing what they would be called upon to undertake, or where.

The final part of their journey was by inflatable rubber boats, which they paddled to the area off the beaches where the obstructions lay, waiting for the invaders. Of the many obstructions that faced the divers, the biggest was Element 'C', which comprised two tons of six-inch steel girder work. Ten feet high and ten feet broad, it was a formidable barrier to the landing craft. The research experiments had found that it required 36 charges, strategically placed, and detonated simultaneously to collapse the structure to a height of some eighteen inches, thus allowing the flat bottomed landing craft easy access over the top of them. The divers also had to deal with pyramid-shaped obstructions, called 'dragons' teeth', and steel girders placed together to form hedgehogs, both types of obstruction having mines fixed to them. Steel girders were laid against fused shells, so that if a landing craft hit the girder, it would strike the cap and detonate the shell. All of these obstructions had to be removed.

The ten units of frogmen, four Royal Navy and six Royal Marines, left the rubber boats and swam to the obstructions. When they submerged, only the inflatable floats carrying the explosive charges were left on the surface. First they prepared lanes into the beaches, wide enough to allow the landing craft access, then moved either side to widen the lanes. The detonation of the charges levelling the obstructions announced their presence, and the enemy responded with mortar, artillery and machine-gun fire. The midget submarines were surfaced, and displayed lights seaward to mark out the landing lanes. As the first wave of troops stormed ashore, the 'frogmen' were waiting for them.

By the end of D-Day, those 120 men had cleared about 900 m (1,000 yd) in length of beach, and removed more than 2,500 obstacles, nearly every one of them mined. They remained to assist in clearing the flotsam that remained after the landings. Equipment and vehicles floundered in the sea, left behind as the war machine surged forward. At the end of the operation which had made the landings possible, they counted the cost: two frogmen dead and ten wounded, some seriously. A remarkable statistic, considering the nature of their operation. They did not consider themselves to be anything other than ordinary men, who had trained for a particular job which they had carried out with precision and faultless determination, regardless of personal sacrifice.

*   *   *

With the landings a success, ports were a top priority for capture, as the mass of stores and equipment needed to sustain the Allied army that now moved through France had to be landed at those ports along the northern French coastline. The enemy in his efficiency had mined the docks, harbours and locks. These had to be cleared, and the task befell a unit designated the 'P' Parties, who were in fact human minesweepers.

Because of the limited quantities of men and equipment pitted against the large area of harbours and docks to be cleared, it was apparent that an efficient and thorough search pattern would have to be developed. To ensure complete safety for ships, every square centimetre had to be covered. Ropes were laid in a box formation, with one movable rope on two opposing sides, thus forming a grid. The frogman would then position himself on one side of the rope, holding it with one hand, he would move his free hand to its full extent, feeling in the mud, and then sweep it back in front of him. He would do this along the length of the rope, until he reached the other end. Another frogman would come towards him on the opposite side of the grid rope, sweeping the other side. They towed a thin rope with a float attached which had two functions: first, those on the surface knew where the men were, and second, the divers could use the buoyed line as a marker when they found an object. When the two men reached their respective ends, they would push the grid rope along the box rope to the full extent of both arms, then move along the grid rope, searching again. This time-consuming but effective method would be used wherever it was felt that a serious danger to shipping existed. Lock gates were booby-trapped, and barges and boats left by the enemy were likewise set to explode if moved. All had to be made safe. Once an area was searched and the finds marked, the sear-

chers moved to the next area, whilst others of the party dived to recover or make safe the mass of shells, bombs and mines.

Those who had volunteered for the 'P' Parties needed to be qualified in the use of the free-swimming frogman equipment, but also needed to know what they had found in the slime and mud below the surface. Special courses were organized for the men, who after an introduction in daylight, were subjected to crawling about with blindfolds on, identifying what they touched, for on the bottom of the docks and harbours they would be able to see nothing.

The first task for the 'P' Parties was with the US forces, whose task it was to secure the port of Cherbourg. This port was vital, as the first support vessels carrying men, material and fuel to the Allies would need to dock there and unload. As in the manner of all the underwater operations, it was completed, and the divers made some interesting finds in the way of new mines. Methods of dealing with them were found, and duly passed on to other units. Once a port was cleared, the particular unit involved would be sent forward to be with the advancing army, so that as soon as another port was captured, the divers could begin their search. Often they were subjected to artillery barages whilst working, and more than one frogman must have wondered, as he submerged looking up at his colleagues, in the see-saw motion of the fighting, which army he would look up at when he surfaced – his own or the enemy's!

With the end of the war in Europe, the task of clearing up began, and defence mines and booms had to be recovered. It was a dangerous job, for some of the explosives had been down for five or six years, and their condition was unknown.

Great Yarmouth in Norfolk was one of many ports now encumbered by defensive mines which had to be recovered. The mines were cylindrical, with two buoyancy tanks, the latter used to aid their laying. The location of the pattern was close to the harbour entrance, in approximately fifty feet of water. During the laying, the connecting cable coiled on each mine unravelled upon lowering into place, and then the vessel moved to the next location.

To recover the mines, the recovery ship moved into location and dropped its anchor, using the tide to move back over the estimated location. The diver, using non-magnetic standard dress, then followed the 'shot line' to the sea bed and began a systematic search. Keeping the rope as near the sea bed and as tight as possible he would move around in a large circle; if the rope fouled on anything, he would coil the rope up whilst following it to the obstruction. It was by this method that the first mine was found.

Each mine had a lifting line, which had to be found by the diver feeling into the mud. When he had done so, the vessel would send down a lifting wire for the diver to attach. Because the mine was part buried, pulling on the wire could not release it from the suction created by the mud. To continue pulling would have parted the wire, or done more serious damage. The answer lay in the services of a fire boat, with its powerful fire fighting pumps and hoses. Because the diver could never have held the hose, with its high water pressure, it was lowered down the wire to the mine, where the diver secured it by rope. Then the hose was secured to the wire at regular intervals. Pressure was applied to the hose, which supplied a powerful force of water washing out the mud. Tension was maintained on the wire, and when the mine broke free, the pumps were stopped. The mine and hose were recovered together. The remaining mines were easier to find, as they were joined by the interconnecting cable.

Chapter 5

Far East operations in the Second World War

In the winter of 1944 a large number of men from the US Navy Combat Demolition Units were sent to England to join the US Forces preparing to invade the shores of Europe. The landings on the beaches of Utah and Omaha were to be headed by the demolition units, who did not anticipate any swimming, as the obstructions to be cleared were exposed at low tide. When the landing craft neared Omaha beach, the enemy directed heavy fire against them. The severity of that fire left debris and wrecked craft, along with heavy casualties, to such an extent that some demolition units were wiped out altogether. Those that remained continued to set up their charges and cleared paths through the defences. The losses on Utah were 30 per cent, and on Omaha about 60–70 per cent. The survivors of this traumatic experience were shipped to the Pacific, where beach reconnaissance and demolition were to be applied in support of future amphibious operations.

*   *   *

Missions of beach reconnaissance for the Americans became standardized after the landings in Europe and the major amphibious operations in the Pacific, and usually took place a number of days prior to a landing, which required the swimmers to remain unseen and unheard, so as not to compromise a possible landing area. With a beach chosen, the swim-mers aboard a landing craft would head into the area and, amid a softening barrage of gunfire from ships and air strikes, the landing craft would run parallel to the beach, with a rubber boat slung outboard on the seaward side. The swimmers then moved into the rubber boat and rolled over the side into the water. In such a manner, a whole string of swimmers could be dropped off, unseen from the beach.

Swimming in to the beach, the men gathered all relevant information regarding water depth and any obstructions and then, the details recorded, moved back out to sea. They would form a long line, a space between each man, whereupon the landing craft would return and make a fast run down the extended line of bodies. A man in the rubber boat held a snare loop, and as the landing craft powered along the line of men, each swimmer held up an arm which was snared in the loop. The momentum of the boat heaved the swimmer out of the water and into the rubber boat, where he would then move into the landing craft, leaving room for the next swimmer.

When hostilities ceased in Europe, the British specialist underwater warfare groups also turned their thoughts to the continuing war in the Far East. In the cooler northern waters, it was the numbing cold that was feared most. Hands and feet were always painfully cold, and neither woollen nor rubber gloves were satisfactory. Body temperature dropped, causing the

UDT/SEALS about to be dropped off for a covert mission, off the Vietnamese coast.

diver to breathe faster, so reducing his endurance. To keep warm they wore all manner of under garments, often to such an extent that it almost restricted their movements. On the plus side, the protosorb chemical used to purify the expired oxygen operated efficiently, being cooled by the surrounding water.

The Far Eastern waters were to produce a reverse situation. High water temperature meant that the protosorb could no longer be kept cool, and the result was to cause sore mouths. The rubber suits worn in northern waters caused the body to overheat. They were discarded and the swimmers wore only swimming trunks with

their diving sets, while face masks were replaced with goggles. As a result the frogmen/swimmers went sick with ear infections and septic cuts on unprotected legs and arms.

The warm waters were the home for a multitude of creatures, which in those days were described more in horror comics than natural history books. The enemy they knew, the job they were to carry out they knew, but the sharks, octopuses, sea snakes and other unidentified creatures they did not. For these reasons, combined with the long distances often involved, free-swimming operations were limited and 'X' craft came into their own, subjecting the frogmen to the water for only limited periods.

Operations by swimmers and frogmen of the COPPs, the Special Boat Squadron and other specialist units were numerous, and the attack on the Japanese cruiser *Takaeo* lying in the Johore Straits in July 1945 was typical. The craft used were the latest type of midget submarine, the 'XE'. Operation 'Struggle' comprised of *XE 1* commanded by Lieutenant J. E. Smart, MBE, RNVR, and *XE 3*, Commanded by Lieutenant I. Fraser, DSC, RNVR.

They were towed to the operational area by the submarine *Stygian*. It had been decided that on this raid the explosive charges were to be fixed to the cruiser's hull by the frogmen, and not dropped onto the sea bed. *XE 3* moved in and located the *Takaeo*, in very shallow water. Moving alongside the heavy ship, Fraser eased the submarine underneath, until it became wedged between the 10,000 ton ship and the hard sea bed. The 39 ton submarine was being squashed as the tide began to fall. Leading Seaman Magennis, the frogman aboard the craft, had dressed ready to set in place the explosive charge. Having flooded the escape chamber he found that he could only open the hatch a quarter of its normal distance. Using a closed circuit breathing apparatus, he could not pass through with the counter lung bag expanded. Magennis deflated the bag which enabled him to squeeze through into the open sea. He made a survey of the ship's hull, and found it to be covered with barnacles and weeds. This would preclude the use of magnets to hold the mines in place. Magennis returned to the submarine to collect a rope, which he used to lash the mines to the hull. It was exhausting work and he was barely able to close the hatch and drain the chamber when he re-entered the craft.

Ian Fraser spent fifty minutes undertaking every possible manoeuvre to extricate the submarine, but to no avail. Then, without warning, it suddenly shot astern, and broke the surface. Fraser immediately flooded the tanks and bottomed the craft. He found that the vessel would not manoeuvre and it was decided that there was a problem on the outside. Magennis dressed in his underwater swim suit and breathing apparatus again. On the outside he found that one of the mine containers had been damaged: after making repairs he returned into the submarine,

allowing Fraser to steam the craft away to rendezvous with the parent submarine. *XE 1* in the meanwhile had suffered a series of misfortunes which precluded her crew setting their charges. Ian Fraser and Leading Seaman Magennis were awarded the Victoria Cross for their exploits, and the result of the attack was that the bottom of the cruiser was blown out.

On another occasion, in October 1945, HM Submarine *Trenchant* moved in to make a reconnaissance of Pucet Harbour, a base for Japanese shipping. In the hours of darkness the submarine surfaced and two chariots were launched. The crews were given a final briefing and given the target heading. They departed the boat and travelled on the surface, then partly submerged through the clear, calm water. Chosing a target the chariots dived and the commander steered his craft on a compass course to bring it under the hull of a large ship. Working quickly, the number two rigged the clips to the bilge keel, then fitted the explosive warhead. Once the charge was in place they made good their escape, having to surface before they were clear, because of a malfunction in a breathing set. They were unobserved and reached the awaiting submarine. The other chariot had also been successful and had returned, and both crews and craft were secured. The submarine dived and moved to a location to watch the results of the raid. Some observed through the periscopes, while others felt the shock wave when it reached the boat. The textbook raid had been totally successful.

It will be seen from the preceding pages that for men to work underwater calls for a special quality, self control and, if the need should arise, self sacrifice. Man under the water is in an alien environment, but those men who carried the name 'frogmen' had not only to learn how to use their equipment, but to improve it, and then write the operations manuals. Training was born from personal experience, and became severe even to the point of ruthlessness, but the end result was unquestionably the best that could be produced.

The frogmen came from a variety of

backgrounds, and most had stable or even mundane jobs before being called for military service. They participated in experiments, gave their points of view, and from them came the two-man human torpedoes, the submersible canoe, the 'X' craft midget submarine, and the much improved and developed diving dress and underwater breathing equipment.

Specialized parachute equipment for dropping equipment and craft into the sea was developed, as were the variety of high explosive charges, time-delay fuses, and devices to prevent the removal of mines once in place. All were designed, produced and perfected so rapidly that, whereas the British were some seven years behind the Italians at the outset of the war, at the end they had not only caught up, but strode ahead to excel with the new fighting weapon, the free-swimming 'frogman'.

Chapter 6
Covert operations

'We dare you to dare', demands the poster depicting free-fall parachutist and abseiling troops of the United States Special Forces, the 'Green Berets'. In the aftermath of the Vietnam war, the need for highly trained and motivated troops to undertake clandestine operations has never been so great as in the 1980s. Their opera-

tional role today is multifunctional, from training partisan forces in the art of guerrilla warfare, to the larger commitment of special forces operation in the event of a major war. In an imaginary scenario of a Soviet Bloc attack against NATO, with vast amounts of artillery fired, masses of tanks coming across the borders, and hundreds of thousands of men advancing, requiring rations and small arms ammunition, the Special Forces soldiers would infiltrate into East Germany, Poland and Czechoslavakia, and even into Russia, destroying supply dumps, air strips, bridges and railway trestles, interdicting the enemy lines of supply, causing unheard of bottlenecks, slowing down the attack, and giving NATO commanders time to hold, reinforce and counter attack. With sufficient well trained, motivated Special Forces soldiers it could be done.

Britain has a dedicated NATO commitment to Norway in the event of hostilities, and as such has military units trained and equipped to operate in that harsh geographical environment, especially in winter. The principal British unit trained in Arctic warfare is 45 Commando Royal Marines, based at Arbroath in Scotland, and they would operate with their supporting units of the Mountain and Arctic Warfare

A British combat swimmer comes ashore after a dive in Arctic waters.

Dutch Marines land in Arctic Norway as part of Royal Marine Brigade forces.

Cadre, Commando gunners, engineers, aircraft and warships. Norway does not allow any foreign troops, even those of the NATO dedicated forces, to be based permanently on Norwegian soil, so to alleviate some of the severe logistical problems, the Commandos leave much of their heavy vehicles and equipment in Norway, making rapid intervention primarily a matter of moving manpower, by ships and air.

If the 'blitzkrieg' should come, and the Soviets were to invade Norway, they would drive south as fast as possible, using Warsaw Pact amphibious troops and paratroops to support the main thrust. Such an assault might not necessarily be the result of an East-West deterioration in relations, but could happen if the Soviets felt that their northern ports and fleet were trapped, or if they saw a definite weakness or break in the NATO alliance. The warning of such action may be limited, but once begun, it

would be the Special Forces of NATO who would have to move quickly to disrupt such an advance.

On NATO's southern flank, Greece and Turkey hold the key to the Soviet's Mediterranean fleet, which numbers some 95 ships, dependent on the political status of the area at any given time, and the number of ships exchanging with the Indian Ocean fleet. The fact is that the fleet, which has its bases in the Black Sea, has to pass through the Bosporus and the Dardanelles, both of which are controlled by Turkey. One problem that faces NATO here, though, is the distrust between Greece and Turkey. They do not have an amicable relationship, and this appears, at times, to be aggravated by Greece's left-wing government. Turkey, out on a limb at the extremity of NATO's reach, is fully committed to the alliance.

The numerous small islands of the Aegean are a haven for SBS covert operations and, indeed, were the proving ground for the first SBS/SAS amphibious operations during the Second World War. The Aegean and its sur-

RM Commando Special Forces being infiltrated ashore in 2 Rigid Raiders.

rounding countries' coastlines do not have severe arctic winters, but have remote, rugged and sparsely-populated stretches of coastline, which expose them to infiltration by skilled operatives in time of conflict. Turkey, like Norway, has a common border with the Soviet Union, and also one with one of her satellites, Bulgaria, which could provide an overland passage for enemy mechanized units, who could secure the narrow channels to allow freedom for their fleet. This would invoke NATO's involvement, and it is here that NATO special forces would use the water to go to the aid of an ally.

In the north, the Soviets could use the severe winter weather to their advantage, as they have a large, efficient and well-equipped arctic-trained army. During such a conflict the NATO special forces would have to operate in extreme conditions, where for the most part sheer survival will be the order of the day. In such a scenario, how would our troops compare to those of their Soviet adversaries? The West's troops are often criticized as being soft, this hav-

ing been brought about with modern living, and this statement is at least partly true.

Up to, and after the Second World War, the soldier was accustomed to hardship, but over the years the developing sophistication of our society and its conveniences have had an effect on the modern soldier; indeed, it has been stated that, even today, the soldier from the 'tougher' north of England is more adaptable to hardship than his southern counterpart. That, of course, does not necessarily make him a better soldier, in so far as some aspects of his role are concerned. However, the modern specialist soldier must now be taught how to live frugally and endure hardship. His counterpart in the Soviet Union will initially be a conscript, and may not be fully conversant with the overall plan of Soviet policy, and as has happened in the past, these troops may well not know where they are. The Spetsnaz, the Soviet's Special Forces, are their élite, they are well indoctrinated, well trained and sufficiently accepted by the hierarchy to be allowed to operate independently, much the same as the Western Allies' special forces.

The Spetsnaz are known to have operated in covert operations from midget submarines, both in Sweden and Norway, using main submarines and larger conventional submarines for reconnaissance of the major areas of interest.

Why are these two particular countries singled out for infiltration, especially as Sweden is a neutral country?

A number of reasons emerge, although only the Soviets themselves know the true answer. The most common theory is that they are seeking places close to the Swedish mainland, where their SSBN nuclear missile submarines can hide, causing concern within NATO regarding its counter-strike philosophy and anti-submarine warfare operations.

A less common theory, although worth considering, is that although Sweden is neutral

Royal Marines SBS train and operate in severe climatic conditions both in water and on land.

and non-aligned, it is not militarily 'friendly' towards Russia and therefore poses a threat which, in a war situation, could need to be neutralized. Sweden's coastal defence relies mainly in mines and fast anti-ship patrol boats. These craft are based among the mass of small islands, where they hide, waiting for targets. Because the channels are narrow and shallow, the Swedes have developed a highly sensitive radar and sonar system which enables these craft to move at high speed in relative safety. In a war, these craft would dash out into the Baltic, strike at the enemy, then return to their bases at high speed, guided by the radar and beacons. These bases along the coastline are guarded by land-controlled mines, which can be detonated if the enemy approaches. There are numerous areas of sensitivity, along with many radar, communications and defence positions, all of which are of great interest to the Soviet Spetsnaz.

Another possible reason for such interest in the Swedish coastline is the fact that Sweden possesses a good road system through to southern Norway, which is where much of the NATO arms, ammunition and manpower would amass in the event of a blitzkreig from the north. The fact that the Polish and GDR Baltic navies alone can muster enough suitable shipping and landing craft to ferry three whole Warsaw Pact divisions across the Baltic in a relatively short period of time gives some support to this theory.

During the period of Sweden's testing of a new wire-guided torpedo, a Soviet 'Whiskey' Class submarine ran aground. It was more than coincidence that they were both in the same area at the same time. The world's press reported the incident, and it was found that the vessel carried nuclear weapons, which were unidentified but could have been in the form of torpedoes, submerged launch cruise missiles, or atomic demolition munitions (ADMs) for Spetsnaz swimmers to carry ashore on covert missions. The submarine also had two attachment points, not normally seen on this class of submarine, and they were thought to be points where midget submarines could be

Part of Sweden's flexible defence comes from the Rangers, Sweden's special forces unit developed to counter Spetsnaz operations.

connected during transportation.

Probably the most sensational Spetsnaz operation occurred within the Stockholm archipelago. This involved six submarines, three of which were midgets, and all had a defined objective. One conventional submarine operated with one smaller craft inside the archipelago, the latter moving into Stockholm harbour, within a very short distance of the Royal Palace. The other two mini-subs entered other restricted areas, where they left tracks on the sea bed.

The Swedish Navy has so far been unable to force any of these vessels to the surface, although they have mounted heavy anti-submarine attacks. The sea bed is considered to be too shallow and the target too small, coupled with the distortion created by the rugged coastline, for conventional sonar to be at all effective.

Added to these incursions, assault swim-

mers have been observed on the beaches and land mass of certain areas, near permanent defence establishments. The tasks the swimmers have been carrying out when observed are classic beach survey and reconnaissance, much as Britain's SBS would do prior to an amphibious landing. The basic difference appears to lie in the fact that our operatives would use the cover of darkness, whereas these alien swimmers have not bothered. The swimmers, having completed their tasks, disappeared out to sea: the Swedish Navy found marks on the sea bed to indicate the presence of a submarine. In one incident a man who was trained to see things in the water (for the area where he worked was militarily very sensitive) saw an object out at sea. His first thoughts were that the object was a seal, but, unsure of his observation, he climbed on to the roof of a building, where he was then able to identify the head of a diver. He then saw another, closer this time, but in line. The closest was some 50 m (55 yd) out to sea, with the furthest at some 100 m (110 yd); looking down to the beach he saw a third diver/swimmer crouched amidst the rocks, holding a rope, which led out to the other two divers. All were dressed in

To counter enemy attacks against any of the small islands, Swedish Ranger Combat Swimmers will undertake underwater infiltration attacks.

black rubber suits, and the third man ashore clearly displayed underwater breathing apparatus, which also was black. The observer noted that the wind was blowing, but it did not affect the movement of the swimmers, who remained in a straight line.

When the swimmer on the beach saw that he was being observed, he moved without any sign of hurry, signalling to the others before entering the water. All swam out to sea where, using their underwater breathing equipment, they disappeared below the water's surface. The observer watched the swimmers disappear, then raised the alarm. No trace of them was found.

It has been stated that some of the Soviet Spetsnaz assault swimmers are defecting Swedish nationals. That may be true, but there is also another interesting angle. During the 18th century King Charles XII of Sweden led an army of some 120,000 men into Russia. The venture was to amass land and what riches could be gained. In Sweden, there was a food shortage, and the economy of the day suffered supporting the venture. The army eventually found itself near the Black Sea when it was forced to surrender. The survivors remained and established their own Swedish community, retaining their customs and language.

During the 1930s the descendants of the former invaders were offered the choice, either to return to Sweden or remain in the USSR. Many went to Sweden, but found the modern society out of touch with their beliefs, as they had not progressed over the years, remaining a separate community. Those who could not settle in Sweden returned to the USSR and the Swedish community on the Black Sea. These people had married within their own community and had retained the Swedish looks and language.

Today those people are fully integrated into the USSR by birth, and would be committed to the Soviet military system; where trained in underwater clandestine operations they could enter Sweden without arousing suspicion, as they would look Swedish and speak the language, thus making ideal *agents provocateurs*.

Chapter 7
The Swimmer Units

A water obstacle in the 1980s, as in the 1940s, is still probably the best medium through or over which to infiltrate and extract covert operations groups and carry out surprise attacks against the enemy, be it in his homeland or behind his forward lines. Much of NATOs northern and southern flank coastlines (like those of our potential enemies) are long, rugged and exposed, creating an extremely difficult area to defend, especially against small groups of highly-trained specialist troops.

Every country of significant size has, within its armed forces, a 'special forces' organization, whose role in war is to carry out reconnaissance missions, raids and acts of sabotage, and to undertake guerrilla warfare operations deep behind the enemy's lines. These units are the élite, and as a matter of course are shrouded in secrecy, even to the point where the Soviet Union does not even admit to having such an organization. In this chapter we shall look at these units world-wide, before examining the more important ones in greater detail.

In Britain the Royal Marines, having the commando and amphibious role, incorporate their past experience into the formidable Special Boat Squadron (SBS). The SBS are limited in

The Royal Marines maintain the Commando and amphibious role and incorporate the formidable Special Boat Squadron, who use canoes as one method of infiltration.

numbers, and although they would probably like to see some expansion, it is doubtful whether they could induct enough suitable members, and even if they could, this would create the usual problems of larger formations in maintaining very high standards. The regular Squadron numbers some 150 members, sub-divided into a Headquarters (HQ) and three operational sections. An additional section is drawn from the ranks of the Royal Marines Reserve (RMR), and numbers some fifty members, who are selected, trained and exercised by their Regular counterparts. The SBS sections are sub-divided into four-man teams, and their principal role is that of intelligence gathering, observation, underwater attack, beach reconnaissance/survey and sabotage. They do not engage the enemy as a matter of course, and cannot normally call on the larger squadron strength, as can the SAS. When needed they can fight, though, and are well equipped to do so, but they will always try to remain unseen.

Since its formation the Special Air Service, which has one Regular regiment and two Territorial regiments, has seen the advantages of using water as a means of infiltrating troops into enemy territory, and has specialist teams formed into 'boat troops'. Over the years, the demarcation between the SBS and SAS boat troops has been the beach head, or high water-line, but today circumstances, and probably unit rivalry, have changed some operational theories. The SAS troops would use water to infiltrate their patrols, who once ashore would depart inland to carry out their operations, also utilizing rivers and lakes for movement and as sources of targets.

The overall objectives of both units are primarily unchanged, but have adapted as the nature of warfare changes. The SAS man will still move inland to carry out his mission, but to arrive he may use a submarine, helicopter or fixed-wing aircraft. Skilled in the use of canoes, Gemini inflatable boats and underwater closed circuit breathing apparatus, his versatility is expanding. The SBS man may also move inland to carry out reconnaissance missions and destruc-

tive raids, he may even be deposited inland, and make his way back to the water to carry out an amphibious task. With these points in mind, it must be seen that, although there is an overlap in role and in operational zones, the SBS are primarily dedicated to amphibious specialization, and are constantly training and experimenting to this end, whereas the SAS use the amphibious capability as part of the overall methods available to deliver its troops to a target area.

Royal Naval combat swimmer dressed in closed circuit breathing apparatus completes training dive.

Although not part of the Special Forces concept, the Royal Navy's professional divers do train for clandestine assault swimming under the umbrella of 'ship attack'. This role is essentially that of a limpeteer, and free swim attacks would be made against enemy shipping. To practise this role, they utilize the Navy's warship facility at Portland, where NATO ships gather to be honed into efficient fighting units, and part of the overall programme is for them to guard against underwater attack. The naval diver will be taken to a drop-off point by inflatable boat, swimming the final stage. After the attack is made, he will swim back out to sea to rendezvous with the boat. Naval divers do not train in parachuting techniques or in escape overland. At one period they were trained in escape and evasion, and combat survival techniques, but today they are not; one reason for this may be the demand on their services in the expanding mine-hunting capability and the manning of deep-diving vessels, leaving the attack swimming to the SBS.

*   *   *

Australia does not have an independent special boat assault swimmer unit, and therefore the role is encompassed by the Australian Special Air Service Regiment (ASAR). Raised in 1957 as a company at Swanbourne, Western Australia, it was expanded to regimental strength in 1964, and blooded in action during the Brunei operations of 1956–66 and in South Vietnam from 1966 until 1971.

Today the ASAR is made up of a headquarters and six squadrons, those being the Base and Training Squadrons, 152 Signal Squadron, and three Operational Squadrons. Training Squadron has six specialist wings, of which Water Operations Wing is just one. Their job is to select and train those members nominated for water operations specialization, who undertake

training in shallow water diving and various skills. Within the Regiment's structure, No 2 Squadron has two Water Operations Troops, made up of patrols of four to six men.

Their role is parallel to that of the British SBS, covering coastline surveillance, reconnaissance and beach survey, reconnoitring likely invasion beaches. Swimming and diving skills allow them to provide sub-surface as well as surface information on beach approaches and the areas immediately beyond. Operations of harassment to demoralize enemy support forces are undertaken, as well as sabotage or destroy missions against such vital targets as shipping in ports, harbour defences and other 'water' targets. Clandestine recovery operations using evasion and escape techniques can be used to covertly exfiltrate personnel or equipment to beach rendezvous, where a rapid water extraction can be made using inflatable boats or canoes and submarines.

Entry into the Regiment begins with the volunteers undertaking a three-week selection test. Those who pass move to the parachute training school to undertake the basic parachute course. They then join the Regiment to begin reinforcement training. Selection and reinforcement combined take approximately nine months to complete, and half the troops will then be trained in basic signals, whilst the other half become skilled in basic medical aid.

At this point, those going into water operations troops attend a basic course, run by Training Squadron. The structure of the course is based around four elements, the first being for small craft handler, the others being three assault swimmer classifications, III, II, I. The full course takes some four to six years to complete, with an assault swimmer class I being capable of planning, conducting and providing advice on all water-orientated operations, including a beach survey or reconnaissance. Regular exchanges are made with other special forces amphibious units in Britain and the USA.

Survival for Australian SAS is important in the outback. A trooper prepares a boar.

*   *   *

Above A heavily-armed craft of UDT/SEALs prepares for an operation in Vietnam.

Above left US Navy SEALs were formed to undertake unconventional warfare in maritime and extraction operations.

Left The SEAL Special Boat Squadron use fast heavily armed craft for insertion and extraction operations.

Within the US Navy there are two Naval Special Warfare Groups, NAVSPECWARGRU ONE in Coronado, California, and NAVSPEC-WARGRU TWO in Little Creek, Virginia. Both have similar establishments, comprising of a SEAL team, two UDT teams, a Special Boat Squadron and an Undersea Warfare Group.

The SEAL (Sea-Air-Land) teams are developed to meet the growing threat of insurgency throughout the world, with a primary mission to undertake unconventional warfare in maritime and riverine environments. The prime mission of the original UDTs (Underwater Demolition Teams) is to support amphibious forces by reconnoitring and clearing prospective landing beaches. As a secondary role they have the capability to support unconventional war-

fare. The Special Boat Squadron's function is to conduct coastal and riverine insertion and extraction operations, for both SEAL and former UDT teams, as well as to provide specialized support for them when required. The Inshore Undersea Warfare Groups are conventional units established to defend harbours, docks and other amphibious objectives from enemy attack, both by surface and underwater. They draw much defensive expertise from the assault SEAL teams.

The UD Teams were phased out in 1983, placing all naval combat swimmer operations under the SEAL teams, who still train for and maintain the underwater demolition role. Men from the UDTs were moved to form Swimmer Delivery Vehicle (SDV) teams, which utilize the vehicles (examined in detail in a later chapter) to carry out beach reconnaissance and anti-shipping attacks. It also befalls the SEALs in the mid-1980s to provide a counter-terrorism team (CT) in the form of SEAL Team Six. This team is controlled by the Commander in Chief of the Joint Chiefs of Staff of the Department of Defense, and is not under CINCLANT Command, unlike the other SEAL teams. The CT team has available considerable operational assets, which include two specially-equipped nuclear submarines, the USS *Sam Houston* and USS *John Marshall*. For the purposes of detailing the operational role, SEALs and UDTs have been identified as separate units.

Each NAVSPECWARGRU has its own forward deployment unit, Naval Warfare Unit One being based in Subic Bay, Republic of Panama, and Naval Special Warfare Unit Two in the Caribbean at Roosevelt Road, Puerto Rico. These units provide training and support for the NAVSPECWARGRUs.

Because of the various organizations and types of mission of the groups, the commanders are dual-tasked, having both conventional and unconventional responsibilities, and with the wide-ranging capabilities involved, they have a variety of chains of command, depending on the mission. Most Lieutenants are qualified in both UDT and SEAL team operations, having completed tours in each, and many of the enlisted men have also served in both teams.

NAVSPECWARGRU TWO is designated the Navy's unconventional warfare planning unit for Commander in Chief Atlantic Fleet (CINCLANTFLT) and Commander in Chief US Naval Forces Europe (CINCUSNAV-EUR). The Commander of the group may join with the unconventional warfare forces of other services to form a joint unconventional warfare task force (JUWTF).

Naval special forces do not have a defined set of tasks or roles, but are a flexible operational arm of the Navy's fleets. It is the approach to a target, either on the water's surface or below it, that distinguishes the Navy's special forces from those of other arms, but whereas water is the basis of their speciality, they also have the ability to operate in other special forces zones. UDT/SEAL teams are more attuned to the fleet, as they are part of the amphibious forces. An example is shown by UDT Twenty, where one platoon of two officers and twenty enlisted men is deployed with the Mediterranean Amphibious Ready Group (MARG). In the Pacific, one pla-

toon is deployed with Amphibious Ready Group Alfa, and a third platoon is based in Coronado, ready to be airlifted to any Amphibious Group which requires specialist forces.

Although the UDT/SEAL teams are mainly concerned with amphibious operations, they do undertake limpet mine attacks against enemy shipping and other waterborne targets. Apart from the amphibious landing role, they will collect maritime intelligence, take photographs, implant remotely-monitored sensors, and deliver weapons to selected targets.

The variety of craft available from the Special Boat Squadrons' inventory support both the UDT and SEAL teams. They infiltrate them using fast craft, they drop off and pick up the swimmers during their beach surveys and reconnaissance missions, and they also provide fire-support vessels and specialized craft required by the SEAL team covert operations.

The Inshore Undersea Warfare Groups provide surveillance and defence on approach beaches, anchorages and harbours against enemy special forces in the form of combat swimmers, mini submarines and assault forces. To undertake this task they use the Mobile Inshore Detection and Surveillance System (MIDASS), which consists of a high-frequency radar and sonobuoys. They also use the Battle Area Surveillance System (BASS) which uses both land and waterborne sensors.

A NAVSPECWARGRU scenario could be divided into three parts, the first being the unconventional warfare phase, where a command and headquarters group would be established in one of the forward operating bases (FOB). The FOB could be ashore or afloat, and would have at its disposal SEAL platoons, a Special Boat Squadron element, and other specialist detachments. The second part would require a SEAL

Above right US Navy SEALs and Army Special Forces meet up on beach diving combined amphibious operations.

Right Once the assault forces have landed, the SEALs will withdraw to carry out raids on secondary beaches.

platoon to conduct reconnaissance missions, clear and mark obstructions, and provide information about the beach, including abnormal currents or surf conditions. Once the assault forces have landed ashore and established themselves on the beach-head, the naval special forces withdraw to be used in other waterborne operations, either on secondary beaches or in river areas.

The SEAL team uses special names for its members depending upon the task that they carry out. The officer in charge is known as the 'wheel'; the 'powder train' carries and cares for the explosives; those leading the 'powder train' and supervising the laying of the charges are 'riggers', and support is provided by the 'swimmer scouts'.

During a demolition raid the team will wait beyond the surf line or clear of the beach. The swimmer scouts will go ashore and undertake a reconnaissance of the beach-head. When the landing zone is determined to be clear, the main force is called in. The beach landing area is defended against surprise attack, and secured for the extraction of the team.

The attack team will move inland, where the powder train will deposit the explosives at the target and allow the riggers to set them up. The withdrawal is made, leaving the swimmer scouts at the target; when the team has left the beach they set the fuses and withdraw to the beach where they depart, leaving the defence party behind. The charges should detonate when all of the personnel are well out to sea.

*   *   *

The most powerful amphibious fighting force in the world is the United States Marine Corps, and within that organization is a small specialist unit, the 'Recon' Marines, who gather intelligence for Marine amphibious units. Force Reconnaissance Company is independent of the Division Reconnaissance Battalion, although this also has Marines trained in the use of inflatable boats and surface swimming, and a small number trained in underwater swimming.

Force Reconnaissance Company has a headquarters platoon, which plans and collates the tasks undertaken. The Supply and Service Platoon provides limited logistic support and is made up of a platoon HQ, supply section, mess section, parachute maintenance and repair section, and an amphibious equipment maintenance section. The Reconnaissance Platoons each comprise three teams, which are subdivided into patrols of six men, and the six platoon commanders are normally employed as task organization commanders for one or more teams. Platoons can be deployed in the small sub-units of six men, or in larger teams, depending upon operational requirements.

SEAL riggers set up demolition charges at an enemy target.

Above Smoke rises above a Vietcong river base during a SEAL raid.

Right US Marine recon divers being recovered after a reconnaissance operation.

The training of a Marine for Force Reconnaissance takes about a year, as they have to learn the skills of amphibious infiltration and reconnaissance behind the enemy's lines, and those who join the company will already have undertaken the thorough and demanding Marine corps training. Water operations are covered in detail, and all of the team members will qualify as divers at a Naval Diving School, and undertake a parachute course which will enable them to make 'wet' drops. Familiarization in the types of boats available and the skill of packing and waterproofing equipment is combined with instruction in the use of boat compasses, metascopes (a hand-carried device designed for locating a source of infra-red rays), and submersible cameras. Each man must be proficient in leaving and entering submerged submarines, and in both open and surf water swimming.

The role of Force Reconnaissance Com-

pany is a flexible one, to undertake deep reconnaissance before and during a landing. The survey of the beach would normally be carried out by SEAL units, but Force Recon can do the job if required to do so. Prior to 'D-day', teams are inserted, either by parachute, inflatable boat, or by swimming on or under the surface to the beach area. Avoiding enemy defences, the teams move inland to seek out defences and reserve forces, and if necessary to call up fire support from ships or aircraft. They carry minimum equipment, and the information that they gather is raw data, which is transmitted to the force commander.

* * *

Left Reconnaissance of enemy defences is part of the 'recons'' role.

Below left Fuseliers Marins, France's green-bereted marine commandos, are introduced to water in various ways.

Below Second Regiment Etranger Parachutiste, the parachute regiment of the Foreign Legion, utilize combat swimmers as a method of infiltration for raiding operations.

France has post-colonial and European defence commitments, and as such maintains two élite units capable of amphibious/swimmer operations. The Fusiliers Marins, France's green-bereted Marine Commandos, are trained in amphibious warfare and employ swimmers who are inserted into beach landing areas before the main assault landing.

The French have a very strong connection with the history of diving, and from this follows their use of covert swimmers trained in the use of closed-circuit breathing apparatus. The selection and training of the commandos is parallel to that of the British and US Special Forces. The other élite unit employing swimmers for covert infiltration is the 2nd Regiment Étranger Parachutiste (REP), the parachute regiment of the Foreign Legion. The regiment is part of France's rapid deployment force, and would spearhead an assault prior to a more conventional troop build up. In the REP's organization it is the 3rd Company that specializes in amphibious operations, and as such they train in the art of wet parachute drops, surface and underwater swimming and the use of small

boats. Using dry suits over combat uniforms, the troops parachute into the sea, carrying their personal weapons and kit in sealed bags, which they then swim ashore with. On the beach, they remove the dry suits, fins and face mask, put on boots, prepare weapons and kit, then move off to undertake the task assigned.

*   *   *

The Royal Netherlands Marine Corps provides assault troops within the NATO alliance. The 1st Amphibious Combat Group is fully integrated in 3 Commando Brigade, Royal Marines. This group also provides divers and frogmen, who are trained at the Mine Counter Measures Service Diving School at Den Oever.

The divers operate from the mine diver boats *Stier* and *Hansa* during mine clearance operations.

These men aid in the defence of ships, harbours and other 'water' targets. They also help in amphibious operations. Company Boat Group have an amphibious section, 7 Netherlands SBS, and are trained for operations under Arctic conditions and integrated in long-range reconnaissance units of 3 Commando Brigade. They are also trained in anti-terrorist actions on oil/gas rigs. Whiskey Infantry Company is integrated in Britain's 45 Commando, RM, and provides the Arctic warfare and survival training for the Netherlands SBS and the Small Boats Group. The Dutch are trained and equipped to work with the British SBS in the Netherlands and in out-of-area operations.

*   *   *

Every ship in the West German Navy has divers aboard. They are full crew members, carrying out all manner of duties, and only dive when re-

quired, to undertake some basic underwater task to keep the ship operational. As with all military divers, they are volunteers, and for those with the desire and aptitude there are full-time opportunities for divers and combat swimmers.

Supporting the basic divers in the underwater maintenance of the Navy's ships are the skilled 'Ship's Divers', who are based at the naval bases and are able to undertake more technical operations, allowing vessels to stay afloat, rather than undertake time-consuming and costly dry docking. Although there are only about 30 of these specialist underwater technicians, they play a vitally important part in the Navy's operations.

Mine divers are a valuable asset in both peace and war. In the latter instance they have the responsibility of defending German coastal areas, as well as of undertaking vital mine clearance operations in the North Sea and Baltic. They operate from their base at Eckernforde and from the Navy's mine sweepers and the Mine Diver boats *Stier* and *Hansa*. In peacetime the divers are often called on to deal with explosives dating from the last war. Exercises with other NATO countries are also a major part of the daily life of the Mine Diver company.

The Combat Swimmers are the equivalent of the British SBS and US Navy's SEALs, and as such are an independent fighting unit within the West German Navy. The Combat Swimmers Company shares the modern military barracks at Eckernforde with the other diver units. The company numbers some 70 men, trained to operate singly, in pairs or small groups, to undertake intelligence gathering or raids against maritime targets. As such the swimmers are trained in underwater swimming, infantry combat, demolition and fast small boat handling.

Although West Germany does not have an amphibious Commando or Marine organization, as part of NATO they may be involved in amphibious operations in the Baltic or Norway, which require combat swimmers to undertake reconnaissance missions, or as an attack force against enemy ships and military installations.

Soviet Spetsnaz combat swimmers form probably the largest force of its type in the world. Photographs are very rare.

Delivery of German swimmers can be by submarine, where submerged 'lock out' and 'lock in' tasks are undertaken by using the vessel torpedo tubes. They also take full advantage of fixed-wing aircraft, helicopters and a wide variety of surface craft, to deliver and extricate themselves.

* * *

The Soviet Union does have a special forces organization, even though it does not admit to it, and it is very active in carrying out subversive missions today. This is Voyska Spetsial' Nogo Nazrachenniya, more commonly known as the Spetsnaz. The total size of the organization is not known, but every Soviet Fleet has at least one Spetsnaz Naval Brigade assigned to it, and as in the case of the Soviet Naval Infantry (similar to Royal Marine Commandos), expansion has been rapid in both manpower, weapons

70

and support equipment over recent years.

While Britain's SBS and SAS in the amphibious role are based on squadron and troop strengths respectively, the Soviets look in terms of brigades, which shows the importance that they attach to the role of covert underwater operations. The Spetsnaz Naval Brigade comprises a Headquarters Company, which encompasses the planning, training and intelligence gathering units; Midget Submarine Group, trained to pilot and maintain the fleet of covert swimmer delivery vehicles; and three Combat Swimmer Battalions, which provide the covert swimmers, whose role includes amphibious assault support to mini submarine raids, and intelligence gathering.

In addition, a Parachute Battalion is used

to secure vital targets inland and to work with the swimmer battalions during behind the lines operations and amphibious landings. Signals and Support Companies, as with all specialist organizations, are vital. In Spetsnaz they are no exception, and are utilized by the other larger units as and when required.

The integrity of the Spetsnaz troops is said to be beyond doubt, but they will still undergo a considerable amount of political indoctrination. Their role means that they will be required to operate independently of the large Soviet formations, and often behind enemy lines, so total loyalty to the country and the Communist party must be paramount.

Within the Spetsnaz Brigade, it is probable that the swimmer battalions, when sub-divided into small units, are assigned to operations with mini submarines and the larger parent submarines for covert operations as well as the am-

Spetsnaz combat swimmer surfaces during operation.

Above Spetsnaz swimmers come ashore after swimming endurance training.

Right Ashore, the Spetsnaz swimmer changes to a combat soldier role to gather intelligence or strike at enemy targets.

phibious landing task groups. The parachute battalion will use parachute techniques to infiltrate enemy territory, and will work in conjunction with the swimmers, for intelligence gathering, raids and inland support of an amphibious landing. Details of low altitude static line parachuting are known, but use of HALO (free fall) techniques are not certain, although they should not be discarded and undoubtedly the Spetsnaz do have teams trained in HALO infiltration methods.

* * *

Southern Africa may be set for the Soviets' next big adventure, and there is evidence that subversive elements are already infiltrating South Africa, landing on remote beaches of the Transkei. The Transkei is an independent state within the land mass of the Republic of South Africa, and has is own black-elected government, headed by a black prime minister. It was the first black-controlled territory, gaining independence in 1963, and is populated by the Xhosa people. A major feature of the country is that it has a border which is part of South Africa's 3,000 km (1,860 mile) coastline, and is therefore susceptible to subversive incursion.

The Republic of South Africa is under threat by communist elements who seek to control the area, and if one takes a very quick and brief look at the reasons, the one point which hits

home is the country's vast mineral wealth. More than 70 per cent of the free world's gold, more than 75 per cent of the world's known chrome, vanadium, platinum, manganese, fluorspar and andelusite are among the long list of minerals available to the West. If South Africa were to fall to the communist onslaught, these and other commodities, invaluable in our technological world, would be controlled by Moscow.

With this in mind, the South African Defence Force is committed to ensuring that the Transkei, along with the other independent black countries within the Republic, are defended and able to defend themselves. The Transkei Defence Force found itself responsible for guarding the seaboard, and so within the naval element a special seaborne unit was formed in 1979. Terrorist subversives are the main target to be repelled, and as it is known that the intruding elements are well trained in the Soviet Union or other Soviet-sponsored camps, the defending force must be equally efficient and well trained.

Right Rapid deployment by high speed boat.

Below right Rapid deployment by helicopter.

Below far right The Seaborne Unit parades in wetsuits and fins.

Below Transkei Seaborne Unit combat swimmers undergo an equipment check.

The Seaborne Unit is trained for rapid interdiction in a water environment and as well as specialist infantry/commando skills, parachuting, helicopter operations and fast raiding craft handling, they are also trained in Scuba diving. Reputed to be one of the best underwater operations units in Africa, it has sound basic training from white officers of the South African Defence Force special forces. Holding the rank of Colonel, the officer who created the Seaborne Unit cannot be identified, but he certainly established the basis for an effective force able to operate from helicopters, small raiding boats, and able to swim both on the surface and underwater, both at sea and in the rivers which abound in the country.

Although it is difficult to stop small-scale terrorist incursions, a larger force landing in the Transkei should find an effective defence awaiting them.

The Special Forces are one of the most specialized and highly-trained formations in the South African Defence Force. Its members are particularly well trained in ways of waging unconventional warfare. This formation is responsible for the reconnaissance of the enemy's territory and the destruction of strategic targets, which are reached on foot, in vehicles, helicopters, across or under water, or by parachute.

The Special Forces Reconnaissance Commandos (or Recces) are organized into naval and military branches, where the former are trained in special forces operations, but also have specialist skills in covert water attacks and reconnaissance from a variety of surface ships, submarines and helicopters. All members of the Marine Recce are trained in swimming and diving techniques.

The role of Recces is one of deep penetration into enemy territory, where they gather intelligence on enemy units and attack strategic targets. They can be the eyes and ears for larger strike forces of heliborne troops, or can guide air strikes against targets. Attacks on ships in enemy harbours, and use of the mighty rivers, encompass the expanding role of South Africa's Special Forces.

Their training is such that they are equally at home on land, in the air and both on and under the water, and they must be able to operate as individuals or in small groups, under difficult conditions with little support.

Before being called up for National Service, all those eligible are supplied with a questionnaire in which they can state whether they are interested in serving in the Special Forces. Those who are interested are drafted to undertake a pre-selection physical, medical and psychological examination.

Candidates who are successful during the pre-selection phase undergo basic training with the Special Forces, which lasts three months. Those who complete the basic training undergo an individual training course which lasts about four weeks, and prepares candidates for the final week, which is 'selection week', and this tests the volunteers to see if they meet the requirements for becoming operational.

Those who are accepted begin the Special Forces' training, which lasts some eight months, where they expand and learn skills that they will require. Suffice to say that these skills are similar to those of all special forces, with added specialist skills such as bushcraft and tracking.

Those who successfully pass through this selection are then classified as Special Forces Operators, and take their place in South Africa's Reconnaissance Commandos.

Most Recces are parachute operational troops, but there is also a naval element, skilled in the defence of marine bases and in covert attacks against enemy maritime targets. For this, they use parachute, submarines and all types of naval vessels to carry the teams into action. Training in the use of closed-circuit underwater breathing apparatus is undertaken with the South African Navy.

With hostile neighbours, South Africa has a unique and highly-skilled strike force which finds itself in action, gaining valuable operational experience.

* * *

Israel produces superior warriors, so it is not unexpected that they should also produce élite combat frogmen. Amongst the specialist combat units in the Tzhal, the Israeli Defence Army, are the Marine Commandos, who in line with similar units of other countries are highly trained specialists in amphibious warfare. The commando unit was formed after Israel's War of Independence, and trained along the lines of the British Special Boat Squadron, using modern equipment and learning specialist techniques.

The unit is built around a small number of troops who are able to undertake assignments in groups, or even as single operatives. Emphasis is on the men getting to the target by different methods, which requires initiative and improvization. Israel has a long seaboard, as do many of her former and present enemies.

To be considered for entry into the amphibious commandos, the volunteer will have completed eleven years schooling and be in very good physical health. Selection covers both physical and technical tests, lasting for one week. The aptitude tests will put the men under pressure and show their ability to function as a member of a team.

Those who pass the selection undertake the arduous twenty-month training programme. Because of the length of time of training, the volunteer is required to sign on for four and a half years' service from the beginning of the course, though many of those who join the unit spend a considerably longer period of service. The training programme encompasses seamanship, swimming, diving, rowing, sailing, small boats, infantry training, parachuting, driving, navigation, survival, communications, explosives, and a non-commissioned officers' course for those not holding officer rank. Upon completion, those who are successful receive the rank of First Sergeant, and join the unit.

*   *   *

Most of the smaller and Third World countries look to the larger powers when it comes to military training and equipment. They look either to the East or the West, depending on the politics of the government in power at the time. Britain today has certain commitments to former colonies, and to others which have aligned themselves to Western influence. The West will, where possible, train and equip those countries within their budget limits, and both government and private arms salesmen will provide new or surplus equipment.

Many countries look to Britain to supply training teams, to create a basis for a Navy, Army or Air Force, and when those countries require more specialized training of either military or security services in the amphibious role, they approach the appropriate ministry and request a training team from the Royal Marines Special Boat Squadron. The SBS may be able to absorb some of these outsiders into their training cadres in the UK but this would open them to a possible security weakness, so they may prefer to do the training in the client's own country. One basic problem is lack of manpower, for both the SBS and the SAS have only limited numbers of men to fulfil their own operational and training requirements.

The client country, provided that its request met with the appropriate ministerial approval, might be guided to one of the private companies specializing in the training and supply of military and security personnel. A programme of training, tailor-made to the particular country's requirements would be developed, and the equipment procured. The team itself would be made up of former members of the SBS or SAS, who with very recent experience could formulate and establish a specialist training camp in the country's homeland, suited to its needs. The team would not be restrained by other commitments and would be able to fulfil the lengthy programme, although its members would still be covered by the Official Secrets Act.

The author knows of a number of companies able to undertake this task, who are highly professional and light-years away from the unsavoury recruiters of mercenaries of past years. These companies work in close conjunction with the government and the military, and undertake a wide range of military and civilian security services.

On the military front, they offer training in areas such as close quarter battle and sniper operations; helicopter tactics; communications and deployment; helicopter weapons systems; bomb-disposal techniques using remote-controlled vehicles; defensive techniques and vehicle security; hovercraft operations; small boat handling and beach reconnaissance; diving and underwater operations; handling and control of submersibles. In the quiet of an office, one can become involved in the world of closed-circuit breathing sets, diving suits, rubber boats and outboard engines that are waterproofed and can be used from submerged submarines, wet parachute jumps, weapons, mini submarines, and swimmer-delivery vehicles.

Not only do covert diver/swimmer opera-tions come to light in military operations, but also in a subject more at home, in the offshore oil and gas industry, where giant steel and concrete cities stand in the vast openness of the North Sea. The men and the oil and gas rigs are highly vulnerable to the whims of terrorists, who once gaining access could pose an immensely difficult problem for the authorities.

Civilian organizations are involved in the studies and subsequent development of offshore security planning, and as such are fully conver-sant with the security threats and the corres-ponding measures that should be observed. They would not be involved in the recapture of a structure, for instance, but in preventing its cap-ture in the first place. At present, however, basic security for the offshore industry is virtually non-existent, staff are not vetted, nor are platforms and rigs made safe from possible terrorist clandestine infiltration.

Chapter 8
Swimmer combat missions

The war in Korea soon found the United States UDT services in action, providing teams for the big amphibious landing at Inchon, charting the harbour, marking shallow water and underwater obstructions and then undertaking nighttime demolition raids against amphibious as well as land targets. UDT swimmers also cleared mines from harbours and rivers, and with elements of 41 Independent Commando, Royal Marines, undertook a number of strikes at enemy targets, often deep behind the enemy's front line.

A lull in operational requirements passed, with no major commitments until the Vietnam war. Thousands of miles of beach needed to be surveyed by swimmers. Two submarines, USS *Perch* and USS *Tunney*, were converted to carry the teams and their equipment to the operational areas, and were kept busy with covert operations, being used by these swimmers in two different ways. One method was swimmer lock-out with the boat submerged, whilst the other was to surface the boat, bring rubber inflatables on to the sub's deck, then submerge, allowing the teams to paddle the boats ashore. With the enemy's lack of radar in many areas, especially in the south, the submarine could surface with little fear of detection. The role of the UDT swimmers was unchanged from that of the Second World War when they reconnoitred beaches and rivers.

The UDT were spread throughout the USA's spheres of influence, and have been instrumental, for instance, in the recovery of US spacecraft which land in the water, and swimmers are also provided for specialist detachments, as in the Arctic, where they train in the art of survival, ice blasting and harbour clearing. NATO was and is an important UDT/SEAL commitment, and in the European theatre of operations they undertake deep dives in support of the Navy's fleets, and carry out swimmer attacks against enemy shipping, as well as their traditional role of beach reconnaissance in support of amphibious landings. All of this is encompassed in the vast amount of training undertaken to maintain the numerous specialized skills required by the swimmers.

Because of the geographical nature of Vietnam, and its vast waterways, it was seen to require a specialized amphibious force capable of undertaking covert operations independent of major commands. The result was the formation of the SEAL teams in 1962 after a personal directive from President John F. Kennedy. The SEALs drew the majority of their members from the UDT; having completed the basic UDT training, selected men continued with specialized training at the Army, Navy, Marine and Airforce special warfare schools. They learned the art of unconventional and guerrilla warfare, combined with waterborne clandestine operations, using free swimming and underwater delivery vehicles. Their tasks include, but are

SEAL teams undertake deep penetration ambushes and strikes against the Vietcong.

not confined to, the destruction of enemy shipping and harbour facilities, and the conduct of reconnaissance missions gathering vital intelligence. They are also able to train and assist friendly countries in counter-guerrilla operations, for which they have vital knowledge, being skilled in the art in the first place. Apart from direct combat or covert intelligence gathering, they provide medical aid and undertake elementary civil engineering projects in 'hearts and minds' operations.

The initial use of SEAL teams in Vietnam was to establish listening posts and ambush operations deep inside Vietcong-held territory. On these missions the SEAL units would usually

insert and extract by small craft which were heavily armed and armoured, and had a shallow-enough draft for access to the limited-depth riverine areas. These first craft were later replaced by custom-designed high speed craft, which were formed into Boat Support Units (BSUs). These, along with Mobile Support Teams (MSTs) and Navy 'Seawolf' helicopters, combined to form a 'SEAL package', which meant that the small SEAL team inserted into enemy territory could call on rapid and effective support when required.

During 1967 the role of the SEAL teams was expanded, and the result was an increase in manpower. A large area of virtually impenetrable swamp and mangrove, named Rung Sat Special Zone, was one other prime area of operation by the SEALs, where the teams carried out ambushes, established listening posts,

The SEALs' strike missions involved the demolition of enemy camps and stores.

and undertook reconnaissance operations and diving. Members of one SEAL team captured a large quantity of Vietcong documents, translations of which showed that the enemy were using a number of freshwater wells in the Rung Sat area. In response, SEAL teams made several highly successful raids against these wells, thus denying the enemy a source of fresh water.

Listening posts set up on the waterways were often manned for seven days, whilst the occupants gathered information about enemy movements as they used the rivers as a prime source of transport. The teams would infiltrate and remain unobserved, with no outside support until withdrawn with their valuable knowledge.

The information gathered was amassed and charted so that SEAL teams using high-speed shallow draft boats could undertake raids and ambushes, accounting for many enemy killed and captured, along with quantities of equipment and valuable documents. In addition to the direct combat role, SEAL members also performed blasting jobs to open up rivers and waterways to allow deeper penetration by naval craft. Their underwater skills were also put to good use in clearing rivers of obstacles, and removing objects from boats' propellers, as well as recovering equipment from downed aircraft. With greater manpower, the role, operations and subsequent results increased.

US Navy SEAL Forward Operating Bases were established on the rivers of South Vietnam. They were heavily defended by crews of naval personnel and SEALs; the latter undertaking patrols for reconnaissance and strikes against the Vietcong and North Vietnamese troops.

It was from one such base, on 10 April 1972, that Lieutenant Thomas R. Norris led a five-man SEAL team into enemy-controlled territory. Using the cover of darkness, their mission was to find and rescue two pilots who had bailed out of their downed aircraft, deep in Quang Tri Province.

The team were lucky to find one pilot, and returned with him to their base before daylight; aboard their base craft they waited for nightfall, when more patrols would go out. But the enemy destroyed the peace and quiet by a concerted attack on the base, using mortars, rockets and machine-guns.

That night Lieutenant Norris led a three-man team up-river to search for the second pilot, but they returned without finding him. A third attempt to locate the man was mounted, again led by Lieutenant Norris, but again this search was unsuccessful. During the afternoon of 12 April, a Forward Air Controller located the missing pilot and was able to give an accurate position. The details were transmitted to Lieutenant Norris aboard the base craft. This time Norris departed the security of the defended base, disguised as a fisherman and accompanied by one South Vietnamese Special Forces operative. They travelled at night aboard a sampan. It was dawn when they eventually located the pilot, who was injured and unable to walk. The two men were able to get the pilot aboard the sampan, where they covered him with bamboo and vegetation. Even though it was daytime, and behind enemy lines they made their way down the river. They were able to evade enemy patrols and it was as they were approaching the base that they came under heavy machine gun fire. They took evasive action and Norris called for an air strike. The response brought fire support on to the enemy area, and a smoke-screen was laid, which allowed the sampan to reach the base without loss.

* * *

Reliable intelligence had determined that important members of the enemy's area political cadre were at a base on an island in the bay of Nha Trang. Lieutenant Joseph R Kerry and his SEAL team were tasked with capturing members of the cadre.

Using small boats, the team reached the island unseen, where they had to scale a 350-foot sheer cliff which placed them above the enemy camp, giving them a tactical advantage, and with luck an element of surprise.

Lieutenant Kerry briefed the team, which split into two groups before moving down a hazardous descent towards the enemy camp. They were successful in their advance, but close to the camp they came under heavy enemy fire.

Kerry was leading the group that came under fire and he caught the brunt of it. A grenade exploded in front of him, causing serious injuries, and leaving him bleeding heavily and in a great deal of pain. Even though seriously injured he directed his group's fire into the enemy camp, and with the radio man alongside him, directed the other group's fire support into the enemy, which took the Vietcong by surprise.

The SEALs won the fire fight, and even though Lieutenant Kerry's wounds had immobilized him, he continued to command the team. Near unconsciousness, he ordered the defence and an extraction site to be prepared and the prisoners guarded. The helicopters evacuated him, his team and the prisoners from what was a highly successful mission. Interrogation of the prisoners provided intelligence of untold value.

* * *

Petty Officer Michael E. Thornton USN was the only American in the SEAL patrol, the other members being South Vietnamese Navy SEALs. Thornton was a US Naval adviser and was involved in intelligence gathering; this mission in October 1972 was to gather information and capture enemy prisoners in an operation deep inside enemy territory.

The team was transported aboard a Vietnamese Navy junk to a drop-off point, where they completed the last leg by paddling ashore in a rubber boat. On land they hid the boat and proceeded by foot towards their objective. During the move they contacted the enemy, coming under heavy machine-gun and rifle fire from a large force of enemy troops. Whilst the team engaged the enemy in a fierce fire fight, they also called for naval gunfire support. They directed the shells on to the enemy emplacements, causing a considerable number of enemy casualties. During the barrage they withdrew to the waterline, to prevent encirclement.

At the waterline the team took stock of the situation and Thornton discovered that the senior officer had been hit by the enemy fire and was believed to be dead. Not wanting to leave the man, if he were alive, in the hands of the enemy, Thornton dashed forward amidst the enemy fire to the officer's last known position. During this action he was confronted by two enemy soldiers, who he disposed of. The senior officer was seriously wounded and upon examination was found to be unconscious. With the enemy closing in on him, he lifted the man on to his shoulders and carried him back to the waterline, where the only way of escape was into the water. He fitted and inflated the officer's life-jacket, and dragged him into the water. He towed him to safety for some two hours before the support craft found them.

These are just three examples of US Navy SEALs actions which typify the type of men in the SEALs. In these three cases the persons named were awarded the Medal of Honor for their individual acts of valour, which were beyond the call of duty.

*   *   *

A combined US Navy SEAL and South Vietnamese SEAL team undertakes fast deployment and pickup training.

A programme of training the South Vietnamese in the special warfare role was introduced, and they were eventually to assume a larger share of the burden, but the SEAL teams still maintained a very active role, and operated alongside the Vietnamese on operations. One operation with fifteen SEALs and nineteen Vietnamese troops undertook a raid, based upon reliable intelligence, into a Vietcong prisoner of war camp. A running gun battle ensued, and a number of South Vietnamese prisoners were freed; large quantities of weapons and supplies were also found and destroyed.

SEAL team aggressive operations accounted for 580 confirmed kills and in excess of 300 probable kills. SEAL team 1 received two Presidential Unit Citations and one Navy Unit Commendation. Its personnel received one Medal of Honor, two Navy Crosses, 42 Silver Stars, 402 Bronze Stars, two Legions of Merit, 352 Navy Commendation Medals and 51 Navy Achievement Medals. SEAL team 2 received the Presidential Unit Citation (Navy) for Extraordinary Heroism in conducting operations into the enemy's strongholds in the riverine environment of the Mekong Delta during the period 1969–71. The team accounted for large numbers of enemy casualties and enemy troops captured, along with weapons, ammunition and documents of immense intelligence value. As with team 1, individuals of team 2 were awarded a wide variety of awards for their part in the unit's operations. All of the awards are symbolic of the gallantry and courage demonstrated by the men of the SEAL teams in their ability to undertake raids requiring the skills not only of amphibious operations, but also of clandestine 'on land' missions.

The United States of America's decision to intervene in the civil unrest in Grenada in 1982 required the services of the SEALs. The role for the SEAL team on Operation 'Urgent Fury', the Grenada mission, was to infiltrate the island and secure the Governor-General's residence and ensure his safety.

The team parachuted into the sea from C 130 Hercules transport aircraft, along with their inflatable boats, which were palleted for the drop. Unfortunately four of the team were drowned during the insertion operation, but with the team aboard the boats, they made for the coastline and in the early hours came ashore

Swimmer Canoeists use canoes to infiltrate enemy coastlines and rivers.

Inflatable boats provide a fast and flexible method of transporting swimmers to target areas.

on the west coast of the island, just north of St George's. Securing the boats, the men moved cautiously inland to Government House, situated in the north-west part of the town. They reached the house and secured it without detection, ensuring the safety of Sir Paul Scoon.

Subsequent assault by US forces developed into fire fights, and the Governor's residence came under attack. The SEALs defended their ground until relieved the following day by the US Marines, whereupon the Governor-General was evacuated by helicopter to the US fleet offshore.

SEAL teams have found a new role, with America's attention focused on political turmoil in Central America. SEAL Military Training Teams (MTTs) have been training selected naval personnel in El Salvador in coastal and river operations, counter insurgency and special warfare tactics. The result has been the creation of a Naval Commando Unit, which in 1982 numbered some sixty men. Today the El Salvador Naval Commando unit numbers some 330 men, including frogmen, base security troops, and men to man the special high-speed support craft.

The role of the Naval Commandos is to stem the flow of arms, ammunition and equipment from Nicaragua, that are being supplied to the Marxist rebels operating in El Salvador. To carry out the ambushes and raids against the enemy encampments, the commandos operate

SBS swimmers will place charges and remove any obstructions in the beach landing area.

swim to the beach. The craft that they have left will remain offshore, armed, ready to provide fire support if it is required. Swimmers moving to the shore line make very small targets, as they search the approach for obstructions, either in the form of man-made defences or natural projections such as rocks, reefs or sand bars. The inclination of the approach is measured to determine the depth of water for landing craft access. The beach clear of the water will also need to be surveyed for vehicular suitability, and will need to have paths cleared of mines and obstructions. Then, moving into the hinterland, they will reconnoitre for enemy troops defences and helicopter landing zones.

In the early hours of 'D-Day' the swimmers will set explosives on any obstructions and set up lights to guide the landing craft into the clear lanes and, on the beach, white tapes to provide corridors through the beach to the cover of the beachhead. The swimmers may take members of the naval gunfire support unit of the commando artillery with them, allowing them to move inland prior to the landing, to direct naval gunfire onto enemy targets.

When searching for suitable beaches and landing areas, or if the swimmers have a speedy task to perform, they may well be taken to the area by submarine, and whilst it remains submerged, lock out using closed-circuit UBAs. The submarine may remain 'bottomed-out', or may depart the area, to return at a predetermined time. The swimmers ashore will need to remain undetected, and once the job is completed they will swim out to sea. Spreading out along a rope, they will await the return of the submarine, which will lock on to the swimmers' transponders then, moving between them with its periscope raised, snag the rope and tow the swimmers clear of the area. Once in a safe area, the men will re-enter the boat.

The swimmers themselves are characterized in many ways but the degree of their motivation can be illustrated by one instance while on an exercise in Northern Norway. Having left the water, the swimmers moved overland on skis to a target area. The route took them over severe

in teams of eight to fifteen men, and in river and coastal operations with the support of fast patrol boats. The units can ambush and strike at targets but currently lack the heavy support often required, although that will change when the new Marine Battalion under training becomes operational.

Britain's Special Boat Squadron still undertakes beach reconnaissance as part of its operational role in the overall amphibious assault plan. Aboard small boats, in the form of canoes or Gemini inflatable boats, they will make an approach to lay off the beach, where the swimmers will then take to the water, and if required, use their closed-circuit underwater breathing sets to

and desolate terrain, far removed from assistance, and on the second day one of the team dislocated an arm. Refusing to be treated as a casevac and carried on a stretcher, he continued for another two days on skis, his arm strapped to his body.

Beaches were reconnoitred at San Carlos in the Falklands by swimmers of the SBS. The swimmers did not lock out from a submarine, but were deposited some distance inland from the beach by helicopter. They moved overland, their underwater swimming equipment stowed in the heavy bergens carried by each man. The beach and approach reconnaissance was only part of the operation, for they set up camouflaged observation posts (OPs) to seek out enemy defences and troop locations. Then, under cover of darkness, the swimmers moved down to the beach area, where they dressed in their underwater dry swim suits and, using UBAs, swam out to sea to begin the survey of the approaches and beaches. Sand samples, beach gradients and any obstructions that could endanger the landing craft were recorded.

Ashore, SBS patrols searched the beachhead and surrounding areas for enemy defences. Photographs could be taken using specialist underwater cameras, and with the other data gathered, the swimmers swam back to the safe beach area and came ashore. Converting yet again from swimmers to soldiers, they would depart inland away from the beach, leaving no trace, their valuable information safe. A rendezvous with a helicopter extracted the team and returned them to a ship offshore for debriefing.

One problem peculiar to the Falklands was the abundance of kelp, which was considered to be a problem factor for the small raiding and landing craft. Prior to the landing, the SBS sections were landed ashore, and from OPs and patrols the dedicated landing beachhead was finally reconnoitred for enemy presence. The all-clear given, the initial assault group of Commandos and paratroops began the run-in for the invasion. Ashore, the swimmers moved to the beach and undertook the task of 'talking in' the landing craft using radios and coloured lights.

The SBS and the SAS endured many days in hides, manning OPs and undertaking patrols to determine the enemy's positions and strengths. Inserted by raiding craft, canoes and helicopter, they gathered information, which was transmitted in short burst transmission and morse signals. Extracted, the swimmers would be de-briefed aboard warships, and allowed to relax briefly, before being briefed and infiltrated again. With the SBS being at maximum numbers in the South Atlantic, and predominantly amphibious, the demands on their services were extreme.

The four-man teams of the SBS can be united if the action demands it, especially for an operation that may require superior firepower, as was the case for the SBS on Fanning Head in the Falklands, when 23 swimmers were involved in one operation, nine General Purpose Machine-Guns (GPMGs) being carried.

All of SBS weapons can be carried in the water, although they will be kept dry if possible. Those that are not needed immediately, for instance the 66 mm LAWs (Light Armour Weapons), spare GPMG ammunition and shot-gun cartridges, are sealed in waterproof bags, as they are susceptible to the effects of water over a period of time. Shot-gun cartridges can be dipped in latex to be waterproofed. All weapons submerged either in salt-water or fresh water will need cleaning at the earliest opportunity, but provided the water is drained, they can be fired wet. In the extreme cold of Northern Norway, however, care must be taken to keep weapons and magazines clear of water, for it will freeze, rendering them unusable.

We have seen that the tasks delegated to both the SBS and the SAS do overlap somewhat, and, for instance, an SBS swimmer team could well find itself carrying a laser target designator to an OP overlooking an enemy target. This is especially useful at an amphibious landing site where a covert swimmer operation may not be practical. The system can be set up and aimed at a target, and when ready a quick burst transmission or high-speed morse message will be sent using specialized radio equipment. At the predetermined time, the designator will be activated, whilst aiming at the target. The strike aircraft will arrive in the target area, flying at extremely low level and at high speed and deliver the weapon. Free from the carrier aircraft, which will make good its escape, the weapon will search for the laser beam reflected from the target, and then lock it into the seeker head. The nose mounted computer assimilates the information and controls the weapon's fins to guide it to the target. After the weapon has struck the target, the team can photograph the results and then, under cover of darkness, exit the area themselves.

In the Soviet Union the midget submarine plays a very important part in the overall concept of Spetsnaz operations, but the swimmer brigades also provide frogmen who can use the other craft to infiltrate enemy coastlines under cover of darkness to carry out reconnaissance and combat missions. The specialized parachute battalion is able to drop swimmers into areas that may be operationally inaccessible to seaborne units. Spetsnaz swimmers will be used to attack vital targets, and are trained in the art of demolition.

It is reported that Spetsnaz swimmers can also carry atomic demolition munitions (ADMs) which could be used in attacks against large targets such as port facilities, airfields and bridge complexes. The small ADM weighs some 32 kg (70 lb) and develops a yield of 10 kilotons. It is man-portable and designed for use by specialist clandestine units. With this equipment, and the intensive use of midget submarines, how safe are Plymouth, Portsmouth and Holy Loch, or indeed the major ports of other European countries and the USA?

Each Soviet training complex where diving and specialist underwater swimming skills are taught is considered to be the best by its training staff, and much effort is put into the task of producing divers who are the best. The submarine training centre for the Northern Fleet runs a course which the underwater swimmers and divers attend, which is run in as near battle conditions as is possible without unacceptable loss of life.

The swimmers and divers are taught submarine exiting and entry, and it is interesting to note that they use the boat's torpedo system, which is a complicated process and demands a lot of courage from those locking out. The need to be able to get divers into and out of submerged submarines is the same for all navies, to undertake covert underwater swimmer operations, to make good an escape from a stricken vessel, and to undertake repairs to the boat whilst it remains submerged. The submarine medical service is dedicated to overseeing the personnel during the training, and undertakes experiments of a medical nature in the extremely cold waters of the north.

Being able to operate in extremely cold water is vital to the Soviets for, apart from the Northern Fleet, the Baltic Fleet is also susceptible to being ice-bound. The Red Banner naval base at Leningrad operates a centre for training divers and swimmers to operate in icy waters. Divers are taught to dive through ice packs to a depth of up to 60 m (200 ft) and how to endure the severe cold. Survival techniques are also taught. One of the instructors has personal survival experience as a member of a four-man team who spent 49 days drifting in mid-ocean. He survived to become a graduate of a Naval Academy and serve in the training centre which produces divers and swimmers for the Red Banner amphibious landing fleet and for Spetsnaz.

The centre studies the effects of cold on divers, both in terms of their effectiveness and endurance. Doctors and psychologists instruct the divers and swimmers in how to survive and operate in such conditions, and provide medical assistance if it is required. Apart from the effects of the cold, the swimmers and divers are taught how to enter through the ice pack and navigate below it, using methods that have been developed to enable divers to return to a hole through which they dived, and finding their way in the low light conditions of the polar winters.

* * *

Above A Royal Navy diver plants a limpet device on the side of a ship.

Right Two Royal Navy divers wearing CDBA leave the water, having made an underwater navigation swim.

In the Royal Navy a Gemini will bring in an attack team of swimmers as close as possible to the target from a parent vessel, as naval swimmers are not trained in submarine lock-out techniques or parachuting. In the water, the paired swimmers will swim on the surface towards the target.

The limpet mines they carry weigh some 2.7 kg (6 lb) and this will affect the diver's buoyancy when they clamp the mines onto the hull of the ship, for they will be that much lighter. Each swimmer carries only one mine, which is stowed in the pit of his back. The mines, which of course are magnetic, are thus kept as far away from the divers' compasses as possible, but any slight deviation is acceptable, as the compass bearing to be swum is taken by line of sight on the surface. A package can be made up of five or six mines, and its buoyancy controlled to make it neutral, leaving the swimmer pair to guide the package and handle the swim board, which contains a compass, depth gauge and watch. The enemy will be prepared for some form of underwater attack, though, and may present the swimmers with a few problems, even if they are not aware of their presence. Part of the Royal Navy's warship work-up routine is simulated attack from clandestine swimmer teams, and for the most part the Navy's diving branch provides the swimmers. Aboard each ship, guards keep watch, and if they see anybody they ignite a thunder flash and drop it into the water. This tells the swimmers that they have been seen. Once the attacking swimmers have placed their limpet mines they are supposed to surface and be captured by the ship's crew, who then interrogate them in an attempt to gain information on the whereabouts of the mines and when they are due to detonate. Meanwhile, the ship's own divers will have descended to seek out the planted mines.

For the most part, the interrogation is a fairly formal affair, but if the ships have additional guards from the Royal Marine Commandos, then the swimmers may be in for a more difficult time.

* * *

Use can be made of covert swimmers in any of the seas and rivers of the world, and for deep

A warship's own divers using compressed air equipment will check for limpet mines.

penetration raids, where an underwater attack is feasible it can have many advantages. The use of such raiders is shrouded in great secrecy and often details are sketchy, but when information does become available it shows that success can be devastating, as the following example demonstrates. The location, and the identity of the special forces involved were secret, but can readily be guessed at.

*   *   *

Two troopers lay expertly concealed in the vegetation that was prolific along the banks of the river. Through binoculars they observed the village on the opposite bank. It was not really a village, but rather a collection of huts with a wooden landing stage reaching out into the river's deeper water. Women and children were observed, in what was known to be a base camp for the enemy guerrilla groups. The troopers made careful notes of the villagers' activities, and could see a group of new recruits being trained, as well as others who had ventured on raids and returned to rest. The river was a means of transport for the movement of food and ammunition, and the guerrillas used an old shallow-draft river boat for that purpose; it was long past its useful life, but they managed to keep it going.

The guerrillas, both men and women, seemed to provide a guard, but spent most of the time under some form of shelter, drinking beer smoking and talking. They were armed with Soviet AK47 assault rifles, and wore a mixed assortment of dress. A number of dogs roamed the camp, or sprawled out in shaded areas, and seemed to form the main system of guarding. The troopers noted the boat which was tied up on the end of the jetty, along with two dug-out canoes, all used for movement of men and equipment. The boat was unarmed, but the crew had AKs, which they kept stacked near the canvas-canopied wheelhouse. Both crew and weapons appeared unkempt.

Remaining in the hide was unpleasant, and the troopers were pestered by insects both day and night, while on one occasion they had a nasty experience with a reptile, which could have resulted in them compromising their position. With all of the relevant information gathered, the troopers moved downstream to observe a defence post that guarded the river from possible waterborne attack. They could make out the heavy machine-gun that covered the open expanse of water, and the men who rotated through the post. Again, the guerrillas were relaxed and casual, and the troopers noted a large dog, tied on the end of a rope in such a manner that anybody coming up the river would attract its attention.

After observing the defence post, the troopers moved under cover of darkness back from the river to the clearer grass lands and headed away towards the safety of their own border. The journey was uneventful, and they made contact with a patrol of special forces, who arranged for their withdrawal.

An air strike against the guerrilla camp would have been feasible, but the target village contained something that the authorities wanted, and did not want destroyed at any cost. A long-range helicopter strike force was considered, but this would have required heavily-laden aircraft to fly their maximum range, committing them to danger. In war this is an acceptable risk, but the helicopters would have made too much noise for a surprise attack, so they too were ruled out. An overland assault by a mobile strike force was also impractical, for it would be identified long before it ever reached the camp, and probably be involved in an action that would result in the loss of highly-skilled troops. The one answer that seemed feasible was the use of parachutists who, being dropped at night, could move into position to attack at dawn or dusk. There was still a problem of surprise, for they might be spotted by other villagers who would raise the alarm. Lack of precise knowledge as to the defence of the camp and possible booby-traps was another drawback, and finally there was the problem of how to extract the force after the attack.

The officer commanding the group eventually came up with a plan to parachute two groups into the area. One would be the attack group, and would use underwater breathing apparatus to swim downstream, to surface and attack the camp. Afterwards they would re-enter the water and swim downstream, past the defence post, to rendezvous with the other group, which would be in a supporting role. They would have heavier weapons and inflatable boats with outboard engines which would be used to carry both groups away, clear of the camp and any counter-attack. They would then move to a pre-planned RV, to be picked up by helicopters.

It appears that the immediate reaction by senior staff officers was total rejection of the plan, for many could not immediately accept the idea of using underwater swimmers. But those who are committed to Special Forces operation see the possibilities of such troops and plans if there is a good enough reason, and after long debate the group was instructed to put together details for a mission and submit it for approval. To eradicate the possibility of an operational leak, a very limited number of personnel would be privy to the plan.

The first group was designated number one section, and comprised twelve men who were the best swimmers. All were parachute trained, and had additional skills such as demolition, signals and medical training. The second group, designated number two section, numbered eight men and would man the inflatable boats, as well as providing back up to the strike section.

The group had decided to make one parachute drop, at low level, in an area of flat grassland away from the river and habitation. Also to be dropped would be four inflatable boats, capable of carrying twelve men each, and five outboard motors, one being a spare. Each man would carry small arms of his choice, and a number of fragmentation and phosphorus smoke grenades. With the great emphasis on speed and surprise, the most careful consideration was given to weapons. They needed heavy firepower capability for medium range as well as close quarters. From the armoury available to

them, each man would carry an Israeli-manufactured Galil, in the Short Assault Rifle (SAR) version. It was chosen as the best weapon available, because of its lightness, compactness, and medium range ammunition of 5.56 mm calibre. The Galil SAR has a folding stock and front pistol grip, and is fitted with 35-round magazines. Each man would carry six magazines.

The support section would be similarly armed, but with additional ammunition, except for two men who would carry the Galil Assault Rifle/Light Machine Gun (ARM), fitted with fifty-round magazines, to give more sustained firepower if required. The support group would also carry four LAAWs (Light Assault Anti-Tank Weapon) to be used against any fortified positions.

Each man in the swimmer section would carry an underwater breathing set, a dry suit, fins, weight belt, mask and rubber sealed bags, and there would be two spares of everything. The equipment would be issued to each man and carried in rucksacks, the spare sets being divided between those not carrying the radio, medical kit or grenades. Every man would wear combat kit, but no badges of rank or unit identification would be worn or carried. The waterproof explosives charges would be distributed to each man, and would comprise waterproof satchels, so that they need only be placed and their fuses ignited, to detonate.

A date was chosen, and final preparations made, so that when the group boarded the aircraft to sit amidst the equipment bundles, they were completely ready. Wearing parachutists' helmets, the static line parachutes on their backs, the reserves on the front, and the rucksacks strapped to them, they lifted off from the airfield. The flight plan was devious and was designed to prevent the enemy from identifying or tracking the aircraft. The aircrew's skill was paramount in order to place the aircraft over the target and to dispatch the men and equipment at the right time. The equipment was pushed out of the open door first, the static lines pulling the canopies clear. After the last package had left the aircraft, the men followed in rapid succession.

Men and equipment landed, spread out over an area of flat grassland. The troops moved towards the equipment, where all ranks were accounted for. Parachutes and harnesses were cached and an explosive satchel laid and fitted with an anti-handling and delayed timing device. Carrying their own rucksacks, the men began the task of man-handling the equipment to the river, where the troopers had indicated a good rendezvous.

Throughout the night the men moved slowly through the grasslands and into the lusher vegetation nearer the river. By dawn, all of the equipment was under cover, but they had not yet reached the RV, and the group lay low throughout the daytime. As dusk fell, they continued on their way, and by the end of the second night all of the men and their stores were at the rendezvous alongside the river, hidden in the vegetation. The night of the second day, number one section moved out, with one of the troopers who had earlier reconnoitred the camp and a man from number two section, who would set up an OP at the point from where the camp had first been observed. The remainder of number one section moved upstream, carrying their rucksacks of equipment and underwater breathing apparatus.

By dawn, number one section had gone to ground upstream of the camp, and the two men in the OP scanned the encampment, which was void of any movements as the sun rose above the horizon. The radio operators of each section waited by their sets.

The two men in the OP watched the camp throughout the day, and observed the activity as the guerrillas went about their business. At midday they saw a group of guerrillas gather in the centre of the camp, then move off into the bush, away from the river. They were armed with AKs and carried an assortment of bags and backpacks. They were dressed in a mixture of civilian and military clothing, some wearing plain green uniforms. Those who remained watched them go, then returned to the shade, to drink beer and talk amongst themselves, whilst the women and children worked around the camp. Only one man remained on the boat, lounging under the canvas shelter of the wheel house. The remainder of those from the boat had gone off with some young women. By dusk, the status in the camp had not changed, and the men in the OP transmitted a sitrep to both sections: number one section decided to execute the plan, and the OP group withdrew under cover of darkness to rejoin number two section.

Up river, the strike section had remained under cover in the riverside vegetation. Dressed in combat uniform, with individual modifications, all wore camouflage cream, and blended in with their environment. They kept their rucksacks packed ready to move, and maintained all-round defence. They were unable to cook or heat anything, and no one smoked. Rations were dry and cold, not a problem during the heat of the day. Time passed slowly, as there was nothing for the men to do as they lay and waited. Those in number two section had inflated the four boats and prepared them for use. Their location was well wooded and an area of lush vegetation, which overhung the river. Outboard engines were fitted to the boats, although they could not be tested because of the noise they would make. The men set up the two machine-guns and LAAWs in case they were surprised, or had to go to the aid of section one.

The leader of number one section made his decision as night crept up over them. The moon replaced the sun and illuminated the bushland and the river's surface. The spare equipment and rucksacks were placed in a prepared cache and the senior explosives trooper laid a charge, set with a delayed timer. Each man now had just his weapon, magazines and webbing belt with pouches. Boots were removed, and the rubber, underwater dry swim suits put on over their uniforms. Their weapons could normally be carried underwater without any special preparations, but because of the muddy conditions they expected to encounter, the men put them in thick black plastic bags, which would keep them dry, and most importantly, clean and free of the silty mud, which could have caused a malfunction. Each man carried satchels of explosives which, when ashore, would be handed to the demolition experts; and each checked his diving set. Black hoods of thin neoprene completed the eerie spectacle.

The attack was pre-timed, from getting all the men into the water, to swimming in the slow-moving mass of water to the enemy camp, getting into position, and then 'H' hour, the time the swimmers would leave the water and hit the camp. Men checked the luminous faces of their watches as the hours passed. Then, it was time to go. No words were spoken or orders given, as each man knew what to do.

The leader and three men fitted their diving sets and the belt carrying the pouches of magazines and grenades; then with fins, weapons and explosives satchels, they moved to the water's edge. The other eight men sat on the bank of the river and fitted their fins, and then with care eased into the water. Moving further into the river, stirring mud on the bottom, they paid out a rope, from the leader back to the others. Once the first four swimmers were in the water, the next four moved to join them. In the last group, the radio operator, using his small compact radio, transmitted to the support section that they were on their way. The brief signal of confirmation was received and the radio was stuffed into a bag and put into the cache with all the other non-essential equipment, for it is difficult to swim with kit, even if its buoyancy has been compensated for.

In the moonlight the men crouched up to their shoulders in the murky water, their black suits and camouflaged faces blending with the background of water and vegetation. With the last man in the water, they put their half-masks in place. Each man held the rope in one hand, and his weapons in the other, and when all were ready they moved out into deeper water. As they moved, they adjusted their buoyancy by expelling some of the air trapped in the sealed suits, by venting at the cuffs. The leader set his compass, which was fixed on a small board, along with a depth gauge and spare underwater watch.

The bearing taken, he checked his watch

and disappeared below the surface. The water that had seen twelve heads bobbing on its surface was now smooth and clear of swirling pools as the men, below, moved forward. The leader had virtually no visibility and could only see the compass by holding it close to his face. He could see nothing in front, and the only contact he had with the others was the rope strung out behind him.

As the first men moved through the water, they stirred up the mud on the bottom, which blotted out even the faint glimmer those at the front had. They had difficulty in seeing their watches even when held close to their face masks. The current of the river affected the swimmers as they struggled to keep control, their main contact with the others being the rope.

Section two pushed the four inflatables into the water, hidden under the green canopy, and loaded all of the equipment that they would take. Unwanted equipment was cached, and set for demolition. The two machine-guns were placed in the bows of two boats, and the LAAWs in the other two. The crews manned the weapons, and the outboard engines. With limited numbers they would have a difficult task to give a full back up to the attack team.

The leader eased himself carefully to the surface, his head barely breaking the surface, allowing him to check the position and observe the camp further downstream. The first streaks of dawn had produced a soft lightness. He checked his watch, then submerged below the surface again. Care had been taken with planning the swim, calculating the movement of water and swimming time, but it was a hit-and-miss judgement and relied on surface observation by the leader and other team members as they became detached from the rope.

The next time the leader checked his position he was at the target, and he began to move towards the bank into shallower water. As soon as the mud cleared the men checked their watches, for the final attack was timed. Then the men moved unseen by each other, taking great care with their weapons, as they did not want

Training for underwater war

Right US Navy SEALs can approach a target either on the surface, or below. This two-man team came ashore having made an underwater approach to a beach.

Below A swimmer takes to the water for the final stage of the operation.

Above Members of the SBS undertake beach reconnaissance.

Below Canoeing is a major part of the swimmer canoeist training.

Right French combat swimmers depart a submarine and swim ashore, in training for covert operations.

Above SBS Swimmers have to be able to operate in Arctic conditions.

Left A Royal Engineer diver drops into the water from a Lynx helicopter.

Above An SBS team parachutes on to land with equipment, to move either inland or to the sea.

Below Submarine lock out chamber crew.

Left A Royal Navy SRN4 hovercraft at speed.

Right SEAL riverine operations required the development of fast heavily-armed support craft.

Below right Navy swimmers are recovered into the cabin of a helicopter after an operation.

Below USS *Grayback* provided the SEALs with their special purpose combat swimmers submarine.

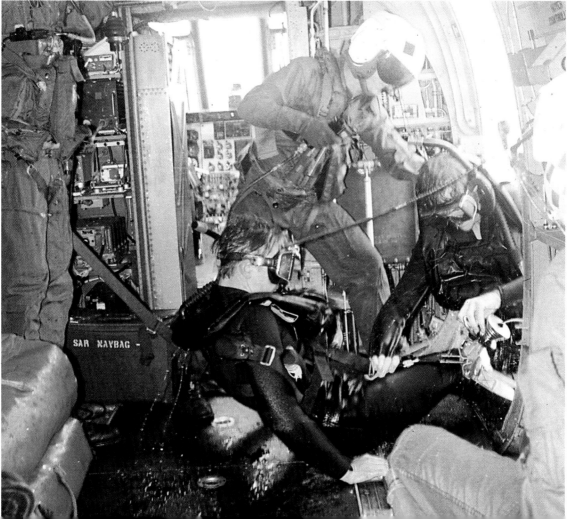

Above The assault team has many methods of re-taking an oil platform; one method is by helicopter and rapid rappelling techniques.

Below A combat support boat provides a high speed diving platform.

them to get covered in mud. With just a small covering of water they lay on the river bed and removed their fins, clipping them on to their belts. They moved to the bank with heads above the water and waited for the signal to move into action.

The camp was quiet as men and dogs slept, in and around huts. The guards lay around the smouldering remains of a fire in the clearing around which the huts were centred. Their AKs, although close, were beyond immediate reach.

Patience is a definite prerequisite for men in the Special Forces, and it was being tested by the twelve men lying in the shallow water. Above them the blood-red streaks of the new day scarred the horizon, the interface between night and day: the time for professional troops to be on guard. As the hands of their watches reached 'H' hour, the men moved forward, allowing them to see the camp. Diving sets were removed and face masks were hastily pushed up onto their foreheads, and plastic bags ripped from their weapons. Moving forward through the muddy bottom, some made firm ground before others, then waited as they quickly assessed the camp layout. Still nothing stirred in the camp.

Safety catches were set to fire, and as the final traces of water dripped from the pouches on their belts, they raised to a crouch and moved forward; each man had a task and knew what to do. As they left the bank they dropped the explosives satchels, which were gathered by the two explosives experts.

The first to awake were the dogs, who gave low grumbling growls, unsure of the intruders, for the water had removed the immediate human smell. Growls gave way to barks, but it was too late, for the first fusilade of fire killed dogs and men, lying by the remains of the fire. In huts, men woke to the noise of gunfire, and groped for weapons, but the Galils put down a devastating fire and huts exploded to the effects of grenades. One of the swimmers move to guard the track from the defence post on the river.

On the wooden boat, the guerrilla stood, shocked at the noise, to be cut down by the accuracy of Galil's fire in the hands of the skilled troops. For the guerrillas, it was a weird sight, to see the men, their enemy, dressed in black glistening rubber suits, and with camouflaged faces. This worked to the advantage of one of the swimmers, as he failed to see the guerrilla appear from behind a bush, but the man, his AK ready to use, stopped to gape at the strangely-dressed troops. The moment of surprise cost him his life.

Fragmentation and phosphorus grenades tumbled into the huts, destroying the enemy and his belongings. Weapons and ammunition were stacked in another hut, built more substantially than the others. Guns, mines, and grenades, all Soviet or East European, were stacked in piles, some new, others old and in need of care and attention. Satchel charges were placed with the weapons and ammunition, in the store huts and on the boat. Other huts burned from the effects of the grenades and firepower of the rifles. When the object of the raid was recovered (what it was remains undisclosed), the signal was given to withdraw, and six men moved back into the water, where they covered the bank with their weapons. They fitted their diving sets, and waited for the next four to join them. Fins fitted, masks ready to pull into place, they all waited in waist-deep water for the explosives experts to ignite the primer cords. Once they were satisfied that the explosives were all right, they moved quickly to the water, breathing from their diving sets. As they waded out to join the others, they pulled their masks down into place. The first explosion was in the food store, and created a large blast and red flash, followed by a heavy black cloud rising into the sky. The swimmers did not wait to see the effects of their work, but submerged below the surface and began to swim downstream.

The men of the support section had listened to the distant small arms battle, and eventually heard the heavy detonation of the explosive charges. The boat drivers pulled on the starter cords of their engines. Three fired and purred into life, but the fourth would not start. It took about ten pulls by a frustrated trooper, who was considering changing the useless engine for the spare buried with the explosive charge, before it fired and roared into life. The engines had been silenced as best they could be, and the enemy would have had to be very close to hear them. Pulling on the overhead branches, the men manoeuvred the boats to the outer green canopy of cover and moved clear of the trees at the water's edge to wait in the clear stream, the engines keeping them in position.

At the defence post the edgy guards possibly saw pieces of wood from their old boat floating past, and fearful of anything unusual, opened fire. The sound of the heavy machine-gun reached the boatcrews, who had not seen any of the swimmers yet, and they presumed that the enemy fire was directed against them. The first boat swept away, its powerful outboard engine pushing it forward in the calm waters. In the bow, one of the troopers crouched holding a LAAW. Rounding the slight bend the boat came into view of the guerrillas, but the machine-gun had been moved to fire upstream. Nothing covered the river downstream. The trooper in the bow of the inflatable boat was ready and as the driver slewed it round to give clearance behind, he fired. The high explosive charge that tracked through the still, warm air was unseen by the terrorists, as was the devastating explosion that ripped into the defended OP. As the weapons fired, the boat driver powered the boat away downstream to join the others.

The boats had moved into mid-stream, one going alongside the twelve heads that bobbed on the surface, and three men moved to each of the boats, handed up their weapons and then were helped aboard. The last men to be picked up were in the boat that had attacked the OP. Once all of the swimmers were aboard, the boats moved downstream in single file. They were able to see the column of black smoke rising behind them, staining the clear blue sky of the new day.

*　*　*

Israel's wars have involved the use of attack swimmers, and although the unit and its opera-

tions are classified, details of two raids have been made public.

*　*　*

Although the sea was calm and only a light wind could be felt, there was a strong current, which made it hard going for the assault force aboard their rubber inflatable boats. Nearing the target the leader gave orders for the assault swimmers to enter the water. Six men put on their underwater breathing sets, prepared their weapons and equipment, and entered the water. Taking a compass bearing, the team submerged and began the swim. The heavy current was a problem, and when the leader broke the surface to obtain a position fix and compass bearing, he found that they were off course. Making an allowance for the current, he set a new course, and submerged below the surface, leading the team towards the target. Their objective was to infiltrate a fortified position and clear a path for a demolition team, who were tasked with destroying a radar station. The fort was manned by Egyptian artillery and commando troops, and was situated on an island at the southern entrance to the Suez Canal. The swimmers were from Israel's Naval Commandos.

Reaching the island, the team surfaced carefully, discarded their underwater breathing apparatus and prepared their weapons for use. The first task was to cut a path through the barbed wire defences which surrounded the concrete wall at water level. This phase was difficult, as the swimmers were standing up to their chests in water whilst cutting the wire, and enemy guards stood above them. When they had cut a path through, they opened fire on the guards standing on the roof of a bunker.

As they opened fire, the fire support unit also engaged the enemy, causing them great confusion. The six-man swimmer team, their swimming equipment discarded apart from their diving suits, moved up the wall, neutralizing any enemy troops they encountered with automatic fire and hand grenades. During this action the leader of the team received a wound in the head, but he was able to continue with the raid. Once the object of the attack was secured, the demolition team was called in, and placed explosives charges in the radar installation. At this point the Israeli swimmers had no losses. Whilst the swimmers were securing their target, other Commandos stormed the fort, engaging the main defending force.

*   *   *

On the second raid the swimmers left their rubber inflatable boat and, laden with mines, swam

into the target area, the Egyptian Naval Base at Ras Sadat. They found two P-183 motor torpedo boats, to which they fixed their explosive charges. They then extricated themselves and rejoined their waiting boat. A second team to be used as a back up had already departed, and they in turn placed their charges on the two boats. They too were able to return to the boat, without detection. Both teams were aboard their raiding craft by the time the explosion indicated that the raid had been successful.

*   *   *

The abbreviated term for France's Marine Commando Fusiliers is 'Groufumaco', and it is

Once ashore the combat swimmers change into combat equipment and link up with local forces.

within that organization that the Hubert commando combat swimmers operate. Numbering 48 men based at Lorient, with an additional fifteen at Toulon, they are all commando- and parachute-trained, and wear the green beret with its badge of a brig, a dagger and the Cross of Lorraine (Free France) set on a shield.

*   *   *

Aboard the submarine, which lay submerged just below the surface, a team of ten commando swimmer divers from France's Hubert Group waited with the boat's crew for the contact with the transport aircraft, which carried another team of swimmers, and orders for the coming operation. Contact was made, and six operational parachute swimmers made the drop into the sea close to the waiting vessel. With the aid of the first team of swimmers they dived down, stowed their equipment and entered the boat.

The short sea passage allowed time for the swimmers to absorb the orders, make plans and prepare equipment. Two nautical miles from an island the submarine stopped, remaining submerged. The swimmer group departed the vessel and swam ashore where, under cover of darkness, they undertook a reconnaissance mission of beaches and vital installations. In the sea the swimmers placed marker beacons near beaches deemed suitable for an amphibious landing. Their mission accomplished, all the swimmers rejoined the submarine, which in turn moved away to join the amphibious force heading towards the islands.

The Independent Islands, the name used for the purposes of the exercise, have a military defence agreement with France, and had been invaded by a neighbouring country, which had disputed ownership for a long time. A call for assistance had been made, and a French amphibious task force was under way to recover control of the islands. The swimmers had gone ashore to gather vital intelligence for the amphibious group commander.

The swimmers joined the ships and passed on the vital information so that an overall plan of action could be decided upon. The Hubert Group comprises the combat swimmers of France's Marine Commandos, who are highly skilled both in underwater missions and in surface strike operations. As the task force drew closer, at some sixty nautical miles from land the men of the Hubert Group boarded PB4s (Zodiac boats with rigged bottoms and two powerful engines, which can achieve thirty knots on a calm sea) and headed towards the islands. Their mission this time was to destroy the island's radar station, and attack defences so as to create a diversion and give the impression that the landing was coming from the west.

The 'Jambert' group followed the markers placed by the combat swimmers and landed on the Eastern end of the island. They held the beach to allow the landing craft to deliver their marines and legionnaires. Another group had selected helicopter landing zones, allowing the Super Frelon helicopters an unopposed landing of troops and equipment. The combat swimmers' intelligence and diversion was vital to the success of the mission.

Chapter 9
Defence and danger

What awaits the swimmers on their missions under the water? Listening devices, anti-personnel charges, turning propellers, high-pitched sonar and coils of barbed wire are all

A combat swimmer makes a small target, even with his head above water, but devices await him.

hazards facing the covert swimmer. Above the surface, guards carrying a variety of weapons search for any give-away traces of attack. On land, guards armed with an ever-increasing array of sophisticated devices seek out intruders, over greater areas, and in total darkness. Elec-

tronic sights, image intensifiers, thermal imagers which give a heat picture of all forms of life, and portable battlefield radar systems complement the barbed wire, mines, sensor devices, microwave fences and guard dogs. All of this means that on land, the swimmer can be blown apart, shot, incinerated in an Astrolite field or savaged by guard dogs (Astrolite is a highly explosive liquid that soaks a few centimetres into the ground. It can be detonated by a sentry or anti-personnel sensor. It has a very short life once laid). But if these defences can be evaded, the success of a raid can far outweigh the dangers encountered.

A warship's best defence is its sonar, which emits a high-pitched frequency which can kill an underwater swimmer. The non-military ship, which is sometimes a better target, with its valuable cargo, can leave its propellers turning, creating a wash along the hull to prevent any swimmers getting close. Small charges can be dropped into the water as a deterrent, for a 0.45 kg (1 lb) charge will kill a swimmer within three metres of the detonation.

During a night attack, the swimmers will submerge for the final part of the mission, having obtained the compass bearing of the target. On a long underwater swim, the tide and current can affect the progress and direction, so periodically the number one swimmer will ease to the surface, exposing only enough of his head to allow the target to be seen and a compass bearing taken, before he slips silently below again to rejoin his companions, before continuing the attack. As they get close to the target, defensive nets or coils of barbed wire could await them, and listening devices may give their location away. They will also be aware of sonar noise and propellers turning, and will have to make a final decision whether to 'go ahead' or look for an alternative target. Above, no bubbling discharge will be seen, and the movement of water with the light reflection from the moon and possibly ships' lights will help hide the swim-

Sentries have to be removed.

mers' presence when they surface to get their bearings.

If the target is a ship, they will move along the hull to the areas affording greatest damage. Charges set alongside the engine room, rudder and propeller shaft will immobilize a ship, even if they do not actually sink it. Enemy divers are likely to be searching the bottom of the ships, and could be encountered, which could result in an underwater fight, followed by anti-personnel charges being dropped. Once the mines are clamped in place and the timers set, the swimmers, now unencumbered by the weight of the mines, take a bearing which will take them out to sea.

Not all the problems faced by the swimmers and attack divers come from the human enemy. The oceans have many inmates below their surface, some harmless, others dangerous, and seeing one of the latter at close quarters is quite disconcerting. 45 Commando, RM provided a small independent amphibious group, of which I was a member, on Perrim Island at the southern end of the Red Sea, and then under the protection of the British garrison in the Protectorate of Aden. The island boasted a couple of fishing villages, a few shops which were like Aladdin's caves, serving not only the indigenous population but also the members and families of the Diplomatic Wireless Station that was the prime reason for Britain's presence on the island. The wireless station was surrounded by a high metal slatted fence and guarded by a variety of soldiers from the regiments who found themselves in Southern Arabia.

Our section occupied a small area on the island, away from everybody else, and our possessions were a Land Rover and a Gemini inflatable boat complete with powerful outboard engine. Our task there is beyond the confines of this book, suffice to say that we often found ourselves over the deep, blue, warm waters, and often in it. It is fair to say that we were all aware of the fact that the Red Sea is the home of the Tiger Shark, and that they had a fearsome reputation. The point came home more when you were in the water, legs dangling below the

surface, waiting to be picked up. We were down at the small jetty one day, and observed a dhow moving towards the landing area. Its stern was low in the water and rope disappeared behind and below the surface. After tying up the dhow the excited crew requested the use of the Land Rover to drag their catch up the slipway. The vehicle was soon in place and a rope attached. Four wheel drive took charge and dragged the unseen catch closer to the surface. As the beast emerged it was soon identified as a Tiger Shark, and very probably one of the biggest ever caught. Up on dry land it was inspected in great detail, especially the mouth. One of the local Arabs found a piece of wood and everybody gathered round to heave on the snout of the monster, opening the vast, gaping jaw, the edge of which was lined with razor sharp incisors that could easily carve a man's trunk in half. Boat work took on a new meaning from that day, as everybody was very wary of the unseen dangers below.

The subject of sharks always makes good dive stories. One such story concerned a group of naval clearance divers who had completed their training and were now members of the Diving Branch. To pass time whilst awaiting draft chits, they went to Falmouth to undertake some further deeper mixed gas and air dives. Upon completion of a day's diving the divers departed to the nearest pub where they devoured a few pints before purchasing some glass flagons of cider. As they left the pub, one of the glass flagons was dropped on the steps outside and before the shattered pieces could be cleared away one of the divers slipped and fell, cutting his arm on the broken glass. Gathering the injured man up, the team took him to hospital where the cut was stitched and bandaged.

The next visit was to the divers' local pub where they knew the landlord rather well. As they entered, and as the first pints were pulled, he asked why the man's arm was bandaged. 'Shark did it', exclaimed one. 'A shark!' retorted the landlord. The divers nodded, and free beer followed, along with an expanding story. By now the press had been contacted and made great haste in getting to the pub to pick up the story. As the free pints were passed on, the story of the two divers was elaborated. They said that, having completed a deep dive, they were on decompression stops when the shark, a large one, came on to the scene. It swam round a few times before making the attack. The diver with the bandaged arm described how he had held up his arm in self defence, and how the shark had bitten him. He went on to describe how his buddy had drawn his diver's knife and stabbed the shark, driving it away, leaving the two divers free to make their way to the surface and get medical help. When the injured man was asked for his name he gave his boss's, the Diving Officer, and the other diver gave his name as that of the Petty Officer Diver. The press departed one way with a dramatic story of a shark attack, whilst the divers departed the other way, having gained a good number of free pints, and an enjoyable evening spinning a yarn to the press.

The following day the national newspapers gave prominance to the shark-attack story, naming the Diving Officer and the Petty Officer as the two men concerned, neither of whom knew anything of the story until it was published. The press sought further details from the Navy, who denied any such attack; meanwhile the Diving Officer had to phone home to convince everybody that he was unmarked and well. The incident caused a great stir, which resulted in the two divers who provided the story getting into a great deal of trouble.

Chapter 10

Selection and training of specialist units

The Royal Navy

Today the Royal Navy's diving training is undertaken at the Diving School in Portsmouth at HMS *Nelson* (*Vernon site*). Courses are run continuously throughout the year, apart from during leave periods. Accounting for all the categories of diver who pass through *Vernon* each year, the numbers average some 450 men. This does not imply a massive diving force within the Navy, but allowing for those leaving the Service, or terminating their diving qualification for some reason, there is a need for continual training, in both basics and the advanced courses for promotion, to replace natural wastage.

The would-be diver has a long way to go before he begins the actual task of underwater training, and even that depends on his passing the initial selection. Life begins in the Royal Navy by initial induction at HMS *Raleigh*, a modern purpose-built shore establishment near Plymouth.

Arriving at *Raleigh*, life is confined to the New Entry block, where the basic art of transforming a civilian into a sailor begins. In comparison to the old hands of bygone days at establishments like HMS *Ganges*, today's newcomer is cosseted, part of the new approach. He will be given an enrolment form and briefed on the types of engagement he can opt for, and the types of jobs he may be suited for. Until this form is signed, the new entrant is not a member of the Royal Navy, and is free to leave. Even having signed the form, he has the option to leave after four weeks. The previous routine where one had to sign on for nine years with no option to leave, apart from discharge by purchase or for other reasons, has gone.

The messdeck (dormitory) accommodates about 25 new entrants, and it is here that they will spend the first week, separated from other new entrants further along in their training. Kit is issued, marked and prepared, and each man is shown how to wear and look after it, which includes washing and ironing. A ship is a confined environment, and it is not the place for untidy or dirty sailors. As with all of the Services, the parade ground looms large at this time, and here the basics are taught. Drill instils discipline, co-ordination and pride in one's appearance. The assault course and physical training come into their own at this point, too. The Navy does not seek to build powerful athletes, but to begin the basics of fitness and aid self confidence. Challenges between teams help to produce a unified spirit and to develop character.

Daily parades transform the rabble into a uniformed, organized body, able to think for themselves, but as part of a group. All military service is based on the foundation of authority and command, and as such a junior rate must obey a senior rate, and they in turn their superior officers, for without this chain of command the system would break down, and in action cost lives.

No introduction to the Navy would be complete without a knowledge of seamanship, and no matter whether the sailor after training will operate computers, cook meals or track submarines, he will at least be made familiar with small boat handling, use of ropes, tying knots and splicing, which no doubt he will soon forget. All new entrants are taught to swim, for it would be no use having a sailor who could not. Towards the end of the six weeks' new entrant period, each man will have an interview, where the results of the education tests and performance assessment during training are formulated and, with all factors combined, the future of the man is determined. It is at this point that those wishing to take up an option in the diving branch will put this forward, and of these,

most will be advised that they will be nominated for diver aptitude selection.

The Royal Navy categorizes its divers as 'trade' and 'non-trade'. The 'non-trade' diver will have diving as a second skill, his first being in any of the Navy's other branches, from steward to electronics technician. All will be volunteers, and the course they will undertake will be for the 'Ship's Diver' qualification. This is the Navy's most basic course, and successful candidates will be qualified to undertake diving jobs as part of a ship's diving team. All HM ships from frigate upwards carry a ship's diving team; mine hunters and specialist seabed ships carry more specialized diving teams.

The candidate for the Ship's Diver course will have to undergo an aptitude selection, for not everybody is suitable to working in an underwater environment. Because the diver spends much of his time alone, often in poor

A trainee diver dressed in dry suit and fins jumping from height.

A diver dressed in dry suit and using Aquarius air diving equipment.

visibility, he must be reliable, intelligent and fit. The tests involve a medical examination, a dry dive to 35 m (115 ft) in a surface compression chamber, jumps from various heights, and distance swims, dressed in an underwater swim-suit (dry suit). The candidate then undertakes dives to 10 m (33 ft) in the Aquarius air diving equipment, and completes limited tasks which are designed to assess whether he can control himself underwater and not panic. This test, lasting one day, will remove those who are totally unsuitable, thus resulting in a good pass rate at the end of the actual course.

The Ship's Diver course lasts for four weeks, during which time the diver will undertake all the drills required to ensure he operates proficiently, using compressed air equipment whilst under the water. Basics such as tying knots are covered, bearing in mind that stewards

Left Two trainee divers with compressed air equipment check the time for a long distance swim.

Below Trainee divers swim in pairs and tow a float so that the instructors know where they are at all times.

and technicians are not seamen. Communication is by way of a rope lifeline, so both diver and attendant must know the signals, and because the diver will be based aboard a ship, he will be taught how to undertake jobs under those vessels. He must get to know the underside, for he will be the underwater watch dog, able to search for explosive devices placed by enemy divers. He will learn the tried and tested search methods required to ensure a hull is 'clean'.

Apart from diving, he will become familiar with the decompression chamber and its use, and he will learn to maintain the equipment he uses under the water. When he completes the course he will return to his ship or shore establishment to continue his normal duties, and

will dive whenever the opportunity arises, for he must undertake 120 minutes' underwater time during each four-month period. Failure to do so results in loss of the 'diver' qualification.

The full seaman sub-branch of diver has been formed from the earlier clearance diving branch, although the term 'clearance diver' still remains. Those in this branch will dive with all types of equipment, and training includes explosive ordnance disposal (EOD). It is open to all new Seaman entries who, after passing through HMS *Raleigh* and successfully completing the aptitude test, can go directly into the 'diver' qualification course. Those men already serving and who have qualified as ship's divers may volunteer to transfer. The aptitude tests for the Diver Branch last five days, and are far more severe than those for the ship's divers. They include mathematical tests, a compression chamber dive to 55 m, physical training, jumps from height into water, long surface swims, fast dressing into underwater equipment, underwater endurance swim, mud crawls and a personal interview. Successful candidates then

Right Stamina is built up during training with divers undertaking mud runs.

Below right Dutch Combat swimmers with a swim board line up the compass to a target before an underwater swim.

Below Two Royal Navy divers in a decompression chamber.

undergo a fourteen-week training course, held initially at *Vernon*, but then at other locations with deeper water and other facilities.

The first five weeks are spent at Horsea Lake, where two weeks are spent on compressed-air diving, with an emphasis on diving techniques and physical exercise. Three weeks are given over to training on the closed-circuit breathing apparatus, using oxygen as the breathing gas. Endurance swims are made along the length of the lake, with physical exercise on the mud runs to build up stamina. The trainee will become proficient with a swim board: this is a board having a compass, underwater watch and depth gauge fitted to it, thus enabling him to observe his target, set a bearing and swim underwater, limiting his exposure to enemy observation to a minimum. During these three weeks, one week is termed 'exercise awkward', when divers are pushed in long swims and called

Left Classroom work shows the diver how to maintain and charge his diving equipment.

Below left The divers move from the lake training centre to the harbour, where they encounter deeper water and currents.

out at all hours to do a variety of tasks, and the exercise is, as the name implies, awkward. For this exercise the volunteers live in accommodation at the lake. For those who do not opt out on the first phase, the next part of the training is at the docks, where for one week the divers are introduced to the nitrox breathing mixture, and are trained in the art of ship's bottom searches and grid searches of docks and harbours.

Portland then becomes home for the divers for two weeks, where they learn the art of seabed searches in deeper water. For the deep training on nitrox breathing mixture, the divers go to either Falmouth or Oban, where they work up to dives to a depth of 55 m (180 ft) on both air and nitrox. The divers return to Horsea Lake for the tool-training, lasting two weeks, and cover other tasks such as propeller and dome changes, underwater cutting and the use of the Coxes bolt gun. The next two weeks will be dry (in the swimming sense), being spent at the Defence Explosive Ordnance Disposal School where they learn the basics of explosives, for demolition and recognition.

The 'diver' on completion of his course will be experienced not only in the use of current div-

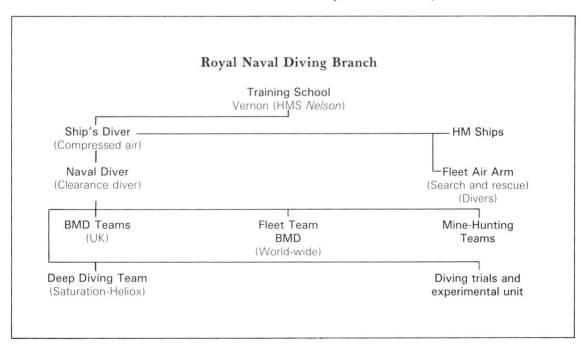

Royal Naval Diving Branch

Training School
Vernon (HMS *Nelson*)

Ship's Diver ——————————————————— HM Ships
(Compressed air)

Naval Diver   Fleet Air Arm
(Clearance diver)   (Search and rescue)
                                                              (Divers)

BMD Teams   Fleet Team   Mine-Hunting
(UK)   BMD   Teams
                          (World-wide)

Deep Diving Team   Diving trials and
(Saturation-Heliox)   experimental unit

Above MV *Seaforth Clansman,* the civilian diving ship chartered by the Royal Navy.

Top HMS *Reclaim,* the Royal Navy's principal deep diving vessel until 1979.

ing sets, but in the use and operation of the decompression chamber, and the maintenance of all the equipment he has to use. He will then join one of the Bomb and Mine Disposal teams located in the United Kingdom. The BMD teams are geared to cover the major ports of Plymouth, Portsmouth, Rosyth, Portland and Clyde, the latter providing divers for Faslane and the nuclear submarines. The team at Rosyth covers Scotland and Northern Ireland, and the team once based at Chatham was phased out in 1974. The new diver may also serve with one of the diving teams aboard a mine hunter. Once he has gained experience in one of the operational teams he can go forward for promotion to a Leading Diver which will involve some sixteen weeks of training, and he can then

EABED OPERATIONS
VESSEL

<small>HMS</small> *Challenger,* the Royal Navy's new seabed operations vessel.

qualify for the Deep Saturation Team.

Deep diving is undertaken from the Navy's sea bed vessel, the first of which was HMS *Deepwater*, later replaced by HMS *Reclaim*. The bell handling was far from satisfactory by today's standards, but a lot of very successful deep diving was carried out. *Reclaim*'s service with the Royal Navy ceased in October 1979. It was planned to replace her with the most modern sea bed vessel possible, but there was a need for a stop-gap vessel, and the Navy chartered the civilian diving ship MV *Seaforth Clansman*: the new vessel, HMS *Challenger*, has undergone two years' extensive trials of new and complex equipment.

The divers trained in deep saturation diving must be flexible enough to accept any new barrier put before them, and in the South Atlantic, they joined the MV *Stena Seaspread*, a

Dynamically-Positioned Deep Diving Support vessel chartered by the MoD, and undertook saturation dives on lost warships in some extremely adverse weather conditions.

One group of divers who were reduced in numbers but are now being re-established, are the Search and Rescue teams. They are recruited from ship's divers and had the function of being aboard the fixed wing aircraft-carriers in the stand-by helicopter. If an aircraft should crash, they would drop into the sea to attempt a rescue of pilot and observer. With the loss of the big carriers their role was drastically reduced, but with the advent of the new type of carrier with the Harrier VTOL aircraft, their requirement has found new life.

Special Boat Squadron

All members of the Special Boat Squadron are volunteers, drawn from the ranks of the Royal Marines, and are qualified Commandos. Long

Left Search and rescue divers are required to be dropped from helicopters, and so train to jump from height wearing equipment.

Below A search and rescue diver drops into the sea from a helicopter during training exercise.

before he begins his selection to become a swimmer canoeist, a candidate will have passed through the Commando Training Centre at Lympstone in Devon, and will have served in one of the Royal Marines Commando Units.

Gone are the Nissen and wooden huts, with their solitary coke stove, sleeping twenty or more men in two-tier bunks. Today, the Commando Training Centre is a modern multi-purpose mass of buildings, centrally heated, and enjoying all modern conveniences. Old hands may look in awe, and mutter about conditions in their day, but although things have changed, the end product is just as hard and tough, and today's Commandos have proved that they can still do the job.

The rate of failure amongst new recruits became very high at one time, as standards were maintained, and to counter the initial wastage in both time and manpower loss, a new system of basic selection is now operated. The Potential Recruits Course gives both sides a chance to look over the other and see if they are suited. Fitness at this point is essential, and with the barest minimum of kit the potential recruit is introduced to the life and what is expected of him. The selectors look for fitness combined with determination and common sense. The fittest of men can shine on general exercise, but when he becomes wet and cold and the pressure is on, he can crack. This is what the Marines are looking for; they do not want those who give up when the going gets tough. Educational tests will assess the learning ability, which is combined with physical training, and an introduction to the weapons a Commando of the 1980s uses. A run of a few miles, followed by some shooting on the range are designed to test determination and skill. Chats about the training and the role of Commandos in the UK defence policy are combined with films to give a broad insight into what could lie ahead.

The Potential Recruits Course lasts three days, and it is on the third day when they get down to the real thing, when the assault course in run, timed and observed. This consists of a

Royal Marine recruits come to terms with water long before SBS training.

number of man-made objects, to develop self confidence and skill in movement, requiring the men to run, jump, crawl and climb. This is followed by a 150 m (164 yd) fireman's carry, again timed. These tests are undertaken whatever the weather, and if it were in the training staff's power, it would be raining. The final test is on the high obstacle course, where the men are tested for determination and acceptance of heights. Commandos abseil from helicopters, climb cliffs and parachute, so a head for heights is essential. On completion of the third day, the potential recruit either wants to come back, or to remain a civilian. They will

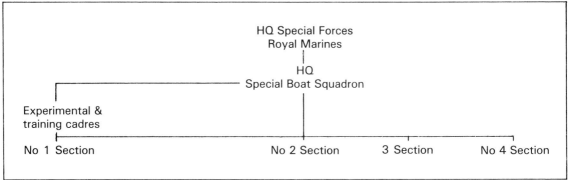

HQ Special Forces
Royal Marines

HQ
Special Boat Squadron

Experimental &
training cadres

No 1 Section   No 2 Section   3 Section   No 4 Section

go home, some with knowledge that they will be called back, others knowing they will not be, either because the selection staff did not accept them or because they have no desire to return.

Those who do return will become familiar with the centre at Lympstone, with its amenities of swimming pool, gymnasiums, all-weather weapons training areas, classrooms and the social area, where dances are held at weekends. The issue of kit and personal weapons is combined with instruction in how to dress and how to keep both kit and weapons

Left Endurance is part of selection, and these Dutch Marine SBS volunteers endure long crawls through mud during week one. Note the fins held in the hand to help stop the body from sinking.

Below Good camouflage is an essential part of SBS requirements.

clean. Drill, for which the Royal Marines are renowned, is a discipline which every recruit undertakes, from basics to the more advanced ceremonial drill.

Physical Training Instructors pursue a demanding programme of body and mind development. Weapons Instructors begin the task of producing a 'soldier', instilling the knowledge of weapons, shooting and basic field craft. The weather makes no difference, and the recruit will soon find himself living rough, learning how to build make-do shelters, cook food, and how to keep himself and his weapon clean. Map reading or cross-country navigation is combined with movement in the field, and the use of camouflage. The assault course becomes familiar as the process continues. Still wearing the blue beret with a distinctive red patch behind the globe and laurel badge of the corps, the recruit will, if he has made the grade,

commence the last three months of his thirty week basic training. Now the physical training and endurance-building programmes will pay off, for he enters Commando training. The tempo increases, and he will have to remember all that he has been taught, and learn the new lessons, forgetting things at his peril.

The weapons not already dealt with are covered in detail, and every man needs to be able to strip and assemble, as well as fire them. Exercises move from Woodbury Common to Dartmoor, and become longer as well as more intensive. The high confidence course, aptly named the Tarzan course, consists of a 'death slide' and a series of different rope bridges, which require a variety of methods to traverse. Finally there is a 27.4 m (30 ft) wall which the recruit has to pull himself over, using a rope. The six-mile endurance course will become more familiar with its mud, water and slime, requiring the recruits to run, crawl and submerge themselves, as they encounter an obstacle. Equipment and rifle are carried, the former holding water and mud to add to the weight.

The Marines have always trained for the old method of getting from one place to another, even with the advent of helicopters, and that is by two feet, or 'yomping'. The speed marches begin with a few miles, and progressively increase in distance, as does the load the men carry. The nine-miler has to be completed in ninety minutes, and the men have to be able to fight when they get to the end. The thirty miles across Dartmoor, carrying full equipment of up to 23 kg (50 lb) has to be completed within eight hours. This march is designed to test endurance and navigation, and is done in groups of three or four men. The final exercise for the recruits is also on Dartmoor, where everything they have learned is tested, and they must endure and fight through a period of night patrols, attacks, ambushes, tracking and simple survival. Those who make

Members of the SBS wear the Royal Marine uniform.

the grade attend a special ceremony, where they hand back their blue berets and accept green berets, becoming active members of the 'green machine'.

'Not by strength but by guile' is the motto of the Royal Marines Special Boat Squadron, whose home base in in the Royal Marines centre at Poole in Dorset. The camp has seen many changes over the years, from the wooden huts of the 1960s to the modern purpose-built establishment of the 1980s. At one time the camp housed those involved in amphibious warfare from all services, but today the SBS and landing craft group share with others from driving and signals companies. The SBS is set aside within this complex of men and buildings, its members for the most part indistinguishable from the other Marine Commandos based at the centre.

Volunteers for SBS selection will already wear the Commando green beret, and will for the most part have served in a Commando unit. They may well have been members of that unit's recce troop, or have served with a raiding squadron, or the Mountain and Arctic Warfare Cadre, or they might have been Marines from a Commando unit's rifle company. The door is open to all those who may meet the basic requirements. One thing is certain, whatever a volunteer's background, he will need to be fit, and well able to use both map and compass. It goes without saying that the candidate will need to be a competent swimmer, and have the right mental attitude required not only for the course but for the job within one of the operational sections.

The candidate's first task is to make a request to his company commander, to attend one of the five two-week SBS selection courses run each year. If he passes this first hurdle he should then be aided by additional training from his unit's physical training and weapons instructors, to enhance his physical abilities and brush up on his map reading. His name will have been forwarded to the SBS at Poole, who will invite him to attend a selection course.

The candidates arrive at Poole and are in-troduced to the role of the SBS. Already the training and selection staff are seeking out the unsuitable, those who see themselves as James Bond, and those who were bored with the unit they were in and sought a change. Once the initial introduction is completed, the candidates are provided with the kit that will see them over the next two weeks, and the demanding rigours of week one begin.

The week begins with the volunteer 'yomp-

The face of determination; the SBS selection process has just begun.

ing', carrying Bergens of some 23 kg (50 lb) in weight, whilst navigating with map and compass over rough ground. The candidate operates alone, and has to make his own decisions as he moves from RV to RV. The volunteer may arrive at an RV to be given a map reference and told to study the route, then after two minutes, the map will be taken away and the man told to carry on. This period of yomping, navigation, sleeping rough and carrying heavy Bergens continues, with the pressure mounting as the days go by, until the final exercise at the end of the first week.

Those remaining, for many will have dropped out either of their own accord or by a decision of the selection staff, will be taken to a hut and told to strip. From their belongings certain items will be returned, and they are then taken to an area where, with what they have, they are told to build a shelter and remain in it for 24 hours, survival being the aim. After this period elapses they will be given their clothes and other items back, plus their Bergens, and sent on a navigation course of thirty miles, across rough hilly ground, to arrive at the coast, where they have to swim out to a landing craft, carrying all of their equipment.

Those who pass this exercise move on to the second week, which is known as diving week. The introduction to diving is done in the swimming pool, on compressed air, and lasts a couple of days. Apart from getting 'wet', the physiology and psychology of diving are covered. The diving soon moves from the compressed air sets to the oxygen closed-circuit apparatus, that members of the SBS sections will learn to use with great professionalism. The introduction to this apparatus is done at Poole, where the murky lake becomes a second home. They then move to Portsmouth and the lake at Horsea Island where the swimmers, using the oxygen sets, swim up and down fixed lines, to gain confidence both with themselves and with the equipment and learn endurance. By the end of his second week each candidate will have undertaken some 500 minutes under the water. They then return to their units, whilst the selec-

tion staff decide who will make the journey back to Poole to begin the course which, if he is successful, will result in a candidate being accepted into the SBS.

The basic swimmer canoeist course is normally run twice a year, although in recent years this has been reduced to once a year, combining all the volunteers into one large group. The course lasts for thirteen weeks, and some forty candidates gather for the beginning. By the half-way point that number is expected to have been reduced to about sixteen, and the selection staff will be extremely pleased if ten men complete the course to enter the squadron. What are the reasons for failure for those who will have already left the course? Some will have had the wrong mental attitude, and when pushed beyond what they thought was possible, given in. Others may have seen themselves in civilian clothes, fitted with a shoulder holster on some covert mission, and could not then come to terms with the gruelling endurance of yomping, canoeing and swimming. Whatever the reason, the SBS lifestyle does not suit everybody, and many soon come to realize this; those who do not of their own accord are rejected by the staff, whose task it is to maintain the extremely high standards. Some are injured during the training process and depart, to return once declared fit, although it may well be on the next course.

The first week of the swimmer canoeist course begins at Poole, where the joining routine and basics, such as signals, are covered, for communications are the life-line and prime purpose of the squadron. The physical side will not be forgotten, but rather than pure slogging on yomps, the emphasis is on doing something constructive. With the first week under their belts, and settled to the task of passing the course, the men move on to a three-week diving phase, commencing with compressed air to regain confidence, and quickly moving on to the oxygen closed-circuit equipment. This is done at Poole and at Portsmouth, in Horsea Lake. By the latter part of this phase the swimmers will also be using nitrogen and oxygen mixtures, which allow them to dive deeper, with a closed system giving off no bubble discharges to disclose their presence. From simple underwater swimming, they are taught underwater navigation using a swim board, as described in the naval section. The techniques of surfacing without a lot of water disturbance, taking compass bearings and moving from one underwater obstacle to another are taught. They learn how to remove equipment and refit it, and how to get in and out of a boat or canoe whilst dressed in swim gear.

Those who pass this phase move to Scotland to join a boat team, where in the Highlands they are taught to use small boats, in the form of canoes, Geminis and raiding craft. The canoe has changed little over the years from when it was first used by the SBS in the Second World War. The Klepper canoe carries two men, and can be dismantled to pack into three bags, or kept assembled when it can carry the crew plus 453 kg (1,000 lb) of stores. In the Highlands they will use the sea and lochs to practise their amphibious skills, as well as undertaking exercises in which the crews will carry their canoes over the hills. They will also find out that an amphibious landing in a Gemini inflatable boat does not stop at the beach, and that the boat, fuel, outboard engine and their own Bergens can be carried over the hills. Exercises of paddling, yomping and swimming are endured, and upon completion of this phase, the volunteers return to Poole yet again.

Demolition is another of the Squadron's key roles, for not all of their work involves observation and reconnaissance. The course they undergo at this stage is basic, and its purpose is only to get the candidates familiar with handling and basic setting of explosives. Tactics are the backbone of the Squadron, for every man must be able to move into an OP, remain unseen, and carry out the task for which he is being trained. Building hides, movement, camouflage and the art of recording what is seen are dealt with in depth, and this phase lasts for three weeks. After the 'on land' phase of living underground and moving without being seen, comes a one-week surf course, where the swimmers learn the art of moving through heavy surf in the small boats that they may use, both landing and launching being practised. From the surf, the men return to land and begin the final exercise, which is a test of all that has been learned throughout the course. Until the completion of this exercise volunteers may still be failed, but when finished, they will know their fate, and those who are successful move to the Squadron for the continuation of the course.

The next step for the small group of men is to attend a basic parachute course at Brize Norton, followed by a one week steerable-canopy course, before returning yet again to Poole. A two-week in-depth weapons course, covering NATO and Warsaw Pact weapons, follows, as well as range work, before a man joins an operational section, where he will continue with specialist training courses in demolition, signals, medical and 'water' parachuting. With his section he will learn the skills needed to work from submarines, surfaced and submerged, and to work as a member of a four-man operational team.

One word paramount in the SBS is 'honesty'. Those selected must be totally trustworthy and reliable, for in war an amphibious landing may depend crucially upon obtaining the correct information, and false reports could cause a catastrophe. A volunteer can be extremely fit, an excellent swimmer, powerful canoeist and have a computer memory, but if he is dishonest, he will fail. On a recent course, four men made a good time from one RV to another. They were asked if they had obtained a lift; they said 'no'. Subsequent enquiries found that they had hitched a ride. That in itself was a crime in the eyes of the training cadre, for the men had been detailed a task, and they had managed to take an easy route. The main crime, however, was that when asked whether they had obtained a lift, they falsified the answer. For that they paid the price, failure from the course and return to unit. In the eyes of the SBS, honesty is the best policy.

Special Air Service Boat Troops

Much has been written in recent years about the Special Air Service, and the selection and training of its members has been covered in great depth. The SAS has long accepted the benefits of infiltration by water, and had its own Special Boat Squadron operating in the Aegean during the Second World War. This role was passed over to the Royal Marines when they took over all amphibious operations. The SAS was disbanded after the war, but subsequently reincarnated during the Malayan campaign for inland behind-the-lines operations. This was the beginning of a new era for the Regiment, which developed a wide range of skills to enable them to carry out their new diversified role.

Looking for any mode of transport that would get them to their destination, they saw in the NATO European scene of operations a need to have some form of small boat and amphibious training. The small boats establishment proved to be no problem, for Geminis and canoes were readily available. The need for diving and underwater swimming proved more difficult, as they had no training facilities, nor anybody who could instruct, and even they could not bypass the rules on diving. They then put men through the Army's diving school at *Marchwood*, which was geared to training engineer divers on compressed air; however, this apparatus was not suitable for troopers parachuting behind enemy lines.

Today the SAS uses the Royal Navy's diving school at *Vernon* for training in the use of the closed-circuit underwater breathing apparatus, which means that they can infiltrate calm water areas using the 'no bubble discharge' system. This equipment is light and durable for carrying on clandestine behind-the-lines operations, even if infiltration is by HALO parachuting.

The Special Air Service draws its volunteers from all units of the Regular Army, and from civilian life through the 21st or 23rd SAS Regiments, which are part of the TA. For the volunteer who arrives at Hereford, it is the start of a long hard journey to the final destination, that of being accepted as a member of the Regiment.

Those who pass the selection will be 'badged' and enter the Regiment. Only between five and seventeen soldiers are accepted from every hundred who volunteer. Then another phase begins, for each man is chosen to learn a basic specialist skill, the subjects available ranging from morse signalling to medics or languages; and to be trained in a tactical skill for one of the four sixteen-man troops, whose specialization covers mountain warfare, free-fall parachuting, mobility, long-range land navigation and boat work.

The SAS make their amphibious role a part of their post-selection specialization, and each squadron has a boat troop, of some sixteen men, trained to use water as a means to an end, for infiltration of enemy-held territory using

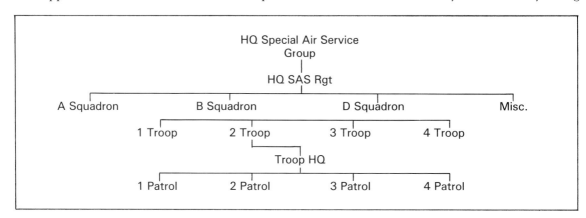

Danish SBS teams are exchanged with British SBS and SAS members for training purposes.

small boats and underwater swimmers.

Wet parachute drops have become an accepted practice, and the skills of using canoes and small boats have been extended. They utilize the Navy's submarines for transporting teams to a target area, where they surface and raft up canoes or small boats to reach land or penetrate up-river to an inland target. They can make good use of lakes and rivers for movement and concealment.

Possibly a problem for the SAS in the amphibious role is the continuous training and maintenance of equipment associated with water operations, and the Regiment's overall commitments in other areas. When the boat troops are suddenly provided with a task they may encounter problems, such as those experienced in the South Atlantic with failure of outdated outboard engines. The Regiment has overcome equipment problems in the past, and will rectify any deficiencies found, all aided by the cross-training and transfer of information with other allied special forces, such as the US Army's Special Forces (Green Berets) and the US Navy's SEALs.

The Royal Engineers

The Royal Engineers are proud of their association with diving, for they can boast the distinction of being Britain's first military divers, and indeed of training the Royal Navy. 1863 was the year that General Sir Charles Pasley formed the first Engineer diving unit, disposing of the wreck of the *Royal George*, using the first heavy standard diving dress.

Today a diver in the Royal Engineers is part of an Amphibious Engineer Unit, and his training begins as a Sapper recruit at Camberley in Surrey, or if joining as a Junior Leader, he would start his career at Junior Leaders Regiment at Dover. The first weeks at Camberley will transform the civilian into a Sapper. Basic training will teach the essential military skills, with a regular quota of drill, weapons training, physical endurance and the

The wreck of the *Royal George* was disposed of by the Royal Engineer divers in 1863.

assault course. Infantry skills are taught, including fieldcraft and shooting, for the Sapper is a combat solider as well as an Engineer, and in the front line he will need to fight and survive. Once the basic soldiering skills are mastered, the recruit moves on to learning engineering tasks. After the training phase, the recruit is able to take his place in a Regiment where the learning process continues. The men of RE face a great challenge, for not only will they operate with the large armoured brigades in Germany, but they could possibly be seconded to one of the independent units who have travelled to the far corners of the earth as remote as the Gilbert and Ellis Islands, Jamaica, Christmas Island, the Pitcairn Islands and Canada, where their full engineering skills are tested. They can also graduate to the adventure skills and train as a combat diver, paratrooper or commando.

Those who volunteer for the role of combat diver will find themselves at HMS *Nelson* (*Vernon Site*), Portsmouth, the Royal Engineers Diving School. There are six basic courses a year, which last five weeks for Royal Engineers, and three weeks for those from the Royal Corps of Transport, Commando Gunners and REME. The reason for the two weeks' difference is that the Engineers learn to use various items of equipment peculiar to their trade. The Special Air Service also undertake their basic air diving course with the Army at *Vernon*, before moving to the Navy's school for more advanced diving.

The Royal Engineer diver is an engineer first, and a diver second. Before being accepted for the diving course all volunteers are put through an aptitude test. This, as with the other

Above Royal Engineer diving involves compressed air only.

Left A Royal Engineer with diving equipment and a mine detector.

services, is used to sort out the 'dead wood' before filling valuable places on the actual course. The course lasts for two days, and the candidate is introduced to the less pleasant side of diving, on the mud flats at low water, and in the murky waters of the river.

Those found acceptable return to undertake the course for the qualification of Army Compressed-Air Diver. The diving school has the mandatory classrooms for the inevitable theory that must be learnt, and a block of showers and changing rooms. Within this complex is a dining room where the food and drink intake of the trainees can be monitored. The living quarters are a short distance away in the main barracks for the port area.

For the initial dives, the school has two diving tanks, one clean and one dirty. The clean one is used to train the diver in the basics of breathing underwater, and clearing his mask. The dirty tank is used for underwater cutting, and here the diver learns to use all the cutting tools available, in murky conditions, for the Engineer does most of his diving in dirty, fast running water, so he must get used to doing things by touch as soon as possible.

The recruit can opt out of the course at any time, of his own accord, or can be rejected by the instructors if he does not measure up. Despite the pre-selection of candidates, they still have a 30 per cent average annual failure rate, although failure is not necessarily the correct term to use, for that percentage includes those who have to leave the course during winter periods due to colds and other illnesses.

The diver will use the standard issue dry suit, rear zip entry, with the Divers Set Self-Contained Compressed Air. This is the same compressed air set as used by the Navy and Royal Marines. To give longer duration on engineering tasks, the Surface Demand system is used in conjunction with the Kirby Morgan Band Mask. By way of familiarization, the divers also have a dive in Standard Diving Dress, which is not in service today.

Those completing the course will be basic air divers, operationally able to dive to 18 m (60 ft) on air. They are able to wear the divers' helmet badge, and receive extra pay for each day that they hold the qualification. To keep 'in date', every diver must undertake a minimum of ninety minutes' underwater during each quarter. The time must be accumulated over two days, and half of the time must be in nil visibility.

Part of the training requires diving in fast-flowing water, for the rivers in which they are likely to work in Germany are fast flowing all of the time. The divers who join one of the Engineer Regiments in Germany receive additional training at Kiel for the operations that they would have to carry out as part of NATO strategy.

Every RE field squadron has a diving team, so the diver could find himself in Germany or down in the sewers in Northern Ireland, searching for weapons and explosives. Teams also operate in more exotic locations, such as Cyprus, Belize and the Falkland Islands. Hong Kong has an active diving team drawn from the Gurkha Engineer Squadron, and in fact the British training team goes to Hong Kong once a year to run a basic diving course for the Gurkha soldiers.

The basic diving course is open to certain overseas engineers units, from countries such as Indonesia, Malaysia, India and Canada. British Independent Engineer units often give much-needed aid to some overseas countries. Among those most recently visited are the Gilbert and Ellis Islands, where EOD operations were carried out; Jamaica, where a training team ran a basic course; the Christmas Islands, where they surveyed the area for a new jetty which is to be built; the Pitcairn Islands, for improvements to their harbour, which required the blasting of a rock formation; Cyprus, for additional facilities to its harbour, and a new Ro-Ro terminal. Even Canada found the Engineer divers at work, constructing the bases for a large bridge across a river; and, ironically, the Engineers found themselves in South Georgia, before the conflict, constructing a new jetty for the Antarctic Survey.

The diver can return to the diving school to undertake the Advanced Army Compressed Air Diving course, which lasts seven weeks, and is primarily concerned with the use of underwater tools and knowledge of underwater construction and destruction. Finally there is the Air Diving Supervisor's course, which for the Royal Engineers lasts three weeks and is for corporals and above, designed to teach divers the role of supervising dives. Other units wishing to have divers on the supervisory course require only two weeks, for sergeants and above, and are restricted to a depth of 18 m (60 ft). These progressive grades also provide for extra pay. The Commando and Parachute Engineers each have a diving team, predominantly trained in EOD and demolition, although the RE divers do not participate in covert operations, unless of course they are selected for the SAS and therefore may well find themselves in boat troop.

The UDTs and SEALs

From within the massive military armoury of the United States of America comes a formidable and élite underwater swimming force, divided by nature of its objectives into distinctive units, each highly specialized. These are the Underwater Demolition Teams (UDTs) and the Sea-Air-Land teams (SEALs). Under a reorganization programme initiated in 1983, all Naval Special Warfare swimmers are organized into SEAL teams, although they still

undertake the same roles, and for the purposes of this book the units have retained their original titles.

Selection for entry to a SEAL team is voluntary, and the same basic course is taken by both groups, and by officers as well as enlisted men. It is held at the Basic Underwater Demolition/SEAL Training department of the Naval Amphibious School, Coronado. The training is open to all members of the US armed forces, as well as candidates from friendly countries. Those found to be medically and mentally suitable join one of two centres, to begin an arduous course that will eliminate those who do not make the grade. The SEAL team combine to number some 200 officers and 1,200 enlisted men. The basic SEAL team consists of 27 officers and 156 men, divided into five platoons.

The first four weeks are tough, starting with two weeks of pre-conditioning training of calisthenics, which begin easy and work up to

US Navy SEALs undergo gruelling training.

Above A SEAL wades through mud, armed with a stoner machine gun.

Right The surf race is designed to create a team spirit.

tion into the role of the SEALs. Volunteers are taught to recognize different types of beaches from the silhouettes of terrain at night or in low visibility. They learn how to produce tactical sketches of beaches, determine conditions of surf and currents, and how to interpret reconnaissance photographs. Specialist training is also given in the use of communications equipment.

Week five is motivation week, and is where the previous four weeks' training is put to the test, in both mental and physical attitudes. Working in small units, the men will undertake exercises in simulated combat conditions. Reconnaissance missions, sabotage raids, establishment of camps and their defence, are combined with competitive races of endurance, team against team, all of which are done in sand, surf and mud. Sleep is brought down to a minimum, and the training teams carefully observe each individual, seeking out those who weaken. Even at this stage of the course, many will fall by the wayside, and return to their previous unit. Those remaining will have passed through the harshest part of the training programme, and will begin the serious business of learning the art of becoming a full member of the SEALs, although termination is still possible. Small boat work begins, and handling soon becomes second nature. The snare fast pick-up is taught and the men are introduced to the different types of underwater

an arduous pitch by the end of the second week. Those who have not opted out or been terminated by the training team, begin the third week divided into seven-man boat crews. This is planned to generate a competitive team spirit. The third and fourth weeks are heavily committed to physical training as well as induc-

Rapid deployment requires SEALs to be trained in rappelling techniques.

diving suits and breathing equipment. Compressed-air scuba diving is followed by the use of closed-circuit pure oxygen systems. Underwater navigation and endurance swims are combined with the use of diver-held sonar and through-water communications equipment. Beach survey and advanced demolitions, both topside and underwater, are taught in detail, and those not parachute-qualified depart to one of the basic parachute training schools to gain their airborne wings.

Those who complete the course are accepted into the unit and join one of the SEAL teams to become a member of the US Navy's Special Warfare Group. They will draw extra pay for diving, handling explosives and parachuting, but will still wear the same uniform as all US Naval personnel, although being identified by special insignia.

Continuation into a SEAL team begins with a thorough grounding in HALO and HAHO (High Altitude Low Opening and High

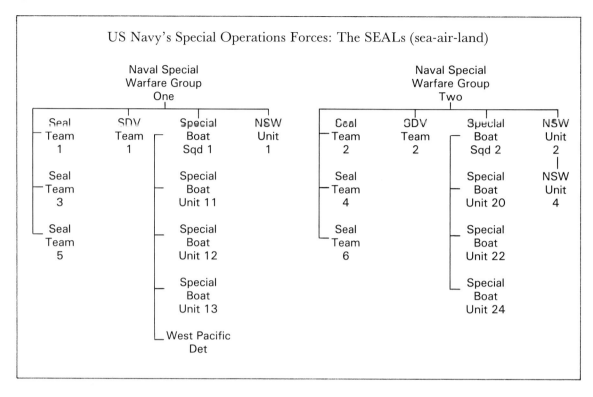

US Navy's Special Operations Forces: The SEALs (sea-air-land)

Naval Special Warfare Group One
- Seal Team 1
- Seal Team 3
- Seal Team 5
- SDV Team 1
- Special Boat Sqd 1
- Special Boat Unit 11
- Special Boat Unit 12
- Special Boat Unit 13
- West Pacific Det
- NSW Unit 1

Naval Special Warfare Group Two
- Seal Team 2
- Seal Team 4
- Seal Team 6
- SDV Team 2
- Special Boat Sqd 2
- Special Boat Unit 20
- Special Boat Unit 22
- Special Boat Unit 24
- NSW Unit 2
- NSW Unit 4

Altitude High Opening) parachuting methods, followed by courses at the Army's Special Warfare School, where the syllabus covers survival, weapons handling (both US and foreign makes), combat medicine, fieldcraft and camouflage, communication and specialized explosive training. Further advanced training is undertaken at the jungle and arctic warfare training centres, all of which combine to produce as an end-product a highly trained and motivated, skilled combat swimmer.

The Green Berets

Who are the US Special Forces Green Berets? They are a unique combination of Ranger, Paratrooper and teacher and are both physically fit and mentally mature. They specialize in communications, intelligence operations, demolitions, weapons and medicine, each man being cross-trained to take another's place in an emergency.

The basic unit of the United States Army's Special Forces is known as the 'A' team. Headed by a captain and a lieutenant, who command ten NCOs, all of whom are cross-trained in skills that enable them to operate under all conditions, whether in jungle, on mountains, in snow or in the desert, an 'A' Team is a complete operational unit.

These Special Forces soldiers are trained to infiltrate deep into enemy-held territory, using advanced parachuting and scuba techniques to locate enemy forces and logistics establishments which might not be locatable by other means. They can report enemy troop movements even when the weather is bad, or without air superiority. With modern communications equipment it would be very difficult, if not impossible, for the enemy to locate the communicators or jam the communications.

SEAL wet parachute training wearing wet suits and fins.

136

The Green Berets have a tradition reaching back to the Second World War, and have been active in the various conflicts in which the United States has found itself embroiled since then. Part of the US Army, they cross-train with other US special forces and those of other nations, such as the British Special Air Service. They are an independent autonomous group whose active role in modern warfare came to the forefront in Vietnam, when they had eleven groups encompassing over 13,000 men (1969). In the period after the American withdrawal from Vietnam, reductions were made, leaving only three groups of about 3,000 men in 1980. Submarines which had been converted for special forces operations were mothballed, and the procurement of the special-operations-capable Talon MC-130 aircraft was forestalled.

During these years of little activity the Soviet Union has continued to expand its Spetsnaz special forces, to the point that today the US government has begun to swing the pendulum back in favour of the Special Forces. Part of the Green Berets' role is to support the Rapid Deployment Force which the US government has established to counter Soviet aggression and expansion into critical areas, where they will also form training teams to assist 'friendly' forces faced with outside agression.

Those seeking to join the élite and attain the coveted Green Beret will first and foremost be a serving member of the US Army, with some three years' experience in another unit. After volunteering for selection, each candidate will be screened for fitness and motivation. Those successful at that stage will enter the Special Forces School at Fort Bragg, North Carolina, to begin a demanding sixteen-week programme, which consists of three separate phases. During the first phase a candidate will operate as an individual, with a critical look being taken at his performance, and it is during this period that the highest percentage of terminations will be expected. The second phase is specialization, where the man will undertake

intense training in specialist subjects. The final phase is to act as a member of a team, where all of the skills taught will be utilized.

Phase one lasts for some thirty days and inducts the volunteer to the rigours of the course and to the Special Forces' lifestyle, for unlike men in the regular Army, the SF soldier is expected to do his tasks with limited orders or without being overseen. He will work alone, and the training team will assess the man's abilities and seek out weaknesses. It is a very physical stage, with marches from six to 25 miles, carrying equipment weighing up to 23 kg (50 lb). Physical training tones muscles and aids in the building of endurance. Basic Army skills are relearnt with a vigour not found in other units. Navigation, camouflage, weapons and survival are the main items on the curriculum, resulting in days that are long and with limited breaks. Any man can leave of his own accord at any time, or be terminated by the training team. The percentage of terminations for both reasons will be in the order of 70 per cent.

The first test for the volunteers is in the form of a week's exercise in the Uwharrie National Forest. The first half is held in the gentler southern part of the forest and is a preliminary work-up, with a culmination of three days held in the rugged northern area. Here the volunteer is dropped by parachute or helicopter, and armed only with the clothes he is wearing plus a knife, he is told to evade his pursuers. He must move unseen, live off the land and above all must not be caught.

Those who pass this phase and who are not parachute qualified attend one of the Airborne Schools where they undertake the US Army's basic parachute training course. Every Green Beret is a specialist and is highly trained in one of four prime subjects, these being Weapons, Engineering, Communications or Medical. The grounding in the subject allocated is the most thorough available, and each volunteer is still under scrutiny, and can be terminated if he does not meet the standards. Those passing this phase move on to the final part of the programme, when the volunteers are formed into 'A' Teams and again parachuted into the swamps of the Uwharrie Forest, where they are hunted by a determined aggressor in the shape of the 82nd Airborne Division, whose sole ambition, through professional rivalry, is to discredit the SF volunteers. Once in the operational area, the teams gather groups of locals, made up of soldiers of a non-combatant variety. They begin the task of forming them into a guerrilla force, which they then lead into an unconventional war against the aggressors. This phase lasts for a month and is the high point of the Green Beret's training, for even here a candidate could still win or lose. At the end of the exercise those who are accepted move on to further and more intensive training, wearing the Green Beret of the Special Forces.

As the role of the Green Berets is to infiltrate behind enemy lines, a number of delivery modes are available to them. Parachuting when practical or possible is a quick and efficient method, using HALO or HAHO techniques, both methods using ram air canopies for stability and accuracy in landing. Water infiltration has developed into a specialized skill and through the training facilities of the SEALs, the Green Beret extends his knowledge of the use of small boats, submarine operations and closed-circuit underwater breathing apparatus. With the combined skills of parachuting, boat work, both surface and underwater swimming, the 'A' Teams have a high degree of infiltration expertise. Apart from sea-borne swimmer intervention, they can utilize rivers, lakes and reservoirs from which to operate or move from RV to RV.

The Spetsnaz

Selection and training for the 'Black Berets' is tough, even by Soviet standards, and is backed by intensive political indoctrination, as they are given privileges not enjoyed by other military

An 'A' team combat swimmer is briefed during diving operations.

units. Initially Spetsnaz personnel are all conscripts, picked by selection centres for service in the Naval Infantry, but they serve for three years rather than the normal two. They can opt to remain after the three years, and if selected for the Spetsnaz would be obliged to do so. Training begins with that of the ordinary Soviet infantry man, but then moves on to specialized tuition in sea and amphibious operations, the latter being based around the concept of the beach assault landing, which is practised in both daylight and darkness, and in all-weather conditions.

Physical training forms a major part of the overall programme, combined with weapons skills, marksmanship and the ability to operate effectively on unfamiliar ground, to produce an above average soldier. The Spetsnaz select only from the best of the Soviet troops, those who can undertake the specialist advanced training involved in establishing the small élite groups. Further training includes learning demolitions, underwater swimming, parachuting and both armed and unarmed combat.

Selection of suitable candidates for the Spetsnaz underwater units begins long before their induction into the Soviet armed forces. Those with the ability and flair are found in the DOSAAF schools (the Voluntary Society for Co-operation with Army Aviation and Fleet), and those who undertake the sub-aqua sportsman route are divided into four groups, the first being for children in the age range of six to nine years. The aim at this stage is to improve their general physical development and teach the basics of sub-aqua techniques. This is the path that leads to the rank of Sportsman 3rd Class. The training at this early stage is important and the instructors are very attentive in seeking out those children who could be of interest to the military authorities. Those who show an aptitude are encouraged to ensure that their full potential is realized, both physically and psychologically.

Skills in Scuba diving are developed at an early age and training for Soviet youth begins in the swimming pool.

The trainees then progress to the next group, which is for ten to twelve year olds, and it is then that their general physical development is worked on more intensively, both in exercises as well as sub-aqua diving. The aim at this point is for the trainees to reach the rank of Sportsman 1st Class.

At thirteen to fifteen years of age, the adolescents transfer to the élite group. Their athletic development is reaching its peak and their underwater swimming ability is improving, both in technical knowledge and endurance. Whilst in this group the trainees go through the stages of 'Candidate for Master of Sport', to becoming 'Master of Sport of the USSR'. The finishing phase of a sportsman takes place in the last group aged sixteen and above, and seeks out the highest sporting skills along with the desired political motivation. The physical capabilities and scuba skills are perfected and the student is prepared to become 'Master of Sport of the USSR, International Class'.

During the years of training teachers have to be aware of the specific characters, of each member's varying abilities and learning curve. Political acceptance and position within the classes are observed. Natural leaders are encouraged from the very beginning.

The DOSAAF Naval School in Odessa is one of the centres where specialized underwater training is given, and at the beginning of the teaching year an initiation ceremony is conducted during the first week. All of the students form up on parade, the school banner is brought out and raised alongside the flag of the Soviet Navy, in accordance with Navy regulations. After a short introduction by the director of the school, the new course members break ranks, one at a time, as commanded by each group's leader, to go forward and read the text of the solemn promise, which of course has been approved by the teaching council and the military authorities. The course member is accepted, congratulated and given a DOSAAF Navy School badge to wear. From this beginning the trainee is made very much aware of the

State's need for divers with special flair, and of the importance and responsibility of the learning ahead, both in diving skills and in the political arena.

The Soviet system places great emphasis on past struggles, and primarily on the enormous losses suffered by the country in the Second World War. Part of the military/political curriculum covers the past, and students constantly meet veterans of the war, many of whom took part in the defence of Odessa. So from the very beginning, the combined efforts of all training staff are based around physical and psychological development.

The school's programme covers both 'theoretical knowledge', and swimming, in pools and at sea, under as well as on the surface. Boat work and specialist underwater training using simulators is undertaken, and one can assume that these 'simulators' include deep diving equipment, decompression chambers and submarine locks and even torpedo tubes. The role of a Spetsnaz diver is far-reaching, and the basic work, such as ships' hull inspections and engineering skills, are well covered; indeed, many of the older students undertaking diver training will already have an engineering skill. In the more advanced training programmes, underwater navigation and photography are among the subjects covered.

The school encourages all trainees to participate in sport, and apart from diving, orienteering, swimming with flippers and underwater endurance swims of lengths of 200, 400, 800 and 1,500 m are undertaken. The water skills are combined with shooting and many other conventional sports, sea rowing and power-boat racing being especially popular. The students are expected to take part in all of the activities within their individual limits.

The instructors, whilst using tried and tested methods of instruction, are always seeking new ways to uphold and extend the resolution of the Central Committee of the Communist Party on improving ideological and politically educational work. The selection of

Above Soviet bloc combat divers work together during some aspects of training.

Top Sea rowing is an important part of training, it builds stamina and develops comradeship.

Above right All phases of diver training are monitored by instructors.

divers to go into the specialist groups within the Soviet Navy is done by a team of naval experts who are attached to the school. They also expand the knowledge of the students in the needs of divers and the specialized tasks they may be called upon to undertake. The students are aware that the naval officers seek out the specially gifted members of their groups. Part of their technique in identifying those with ap-

titude and a dedicated intelligence is to divide the trainees into groups which then compete against each other in sub-aqua and weapons skills. The judges are picked from the school's instructors, and points are awarded for each part of the competition. Diplomas are awarded to the winning team, along with souvenir badges and the traditional prize, a cake. With students beginning a programme of underwater training and political guidance at the age of six to nine years, the Spetsnaz has ample numbers of trained and motivated members to join its swimmer battalions as the youngsters mature.

It is clear that Spetsnaz combat swimmers are picket from the very best that the Soviet Union can produce, and many are chosen from the Naval Infantry (Marines) who already

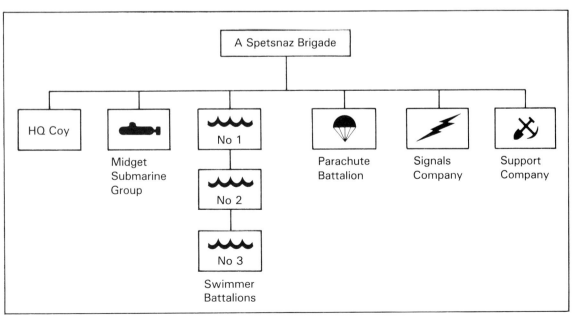

recruit the more superior personnel. They are characterized as having 'hearts full of flaming hatred for the enemy and pride for the Red Navy'.

The crews of the Spetsnaz Midget Submarine Group wear the standard Soviet submariner's uniform, whilst the remainder of the Spetsnaz wear the uniform of the Soviet Naval Infantry, which is a mixture of Army and Navy kit. They also wear the distinctive Black Beret, which in itself is a badge of élitism. In the field, they wear black fatigues and a black bush-type jacket. Calf-length black leather boots and a black belt complete the outer garments. The belt has a buckle which depicts the insignia of the fleet to which the wearer belongs. The neck of the bush jacket is worn open, displaying the blue-and-white striped T-shirt, distinctive to the Soviet Naval Infantry. When in action, the T-shirt is covered by the jacket and camouflaged smocks are worn. The beret is exchanged

for a steel helmet, although like their Western equivalents, the Spetsnaz wear the beret in action. The helmet has a five-pointed star combined with an anchor stencilled on the front in an unobtrusive matt red paint. By virtue of the fact that the Spetsnaz wear the uniform of the Naval Infantry, they can intermix with naval units, blending in, to preserve their anonymity as specialist covert troops.

Combat Engineers

Whilst the swimmers of the SBS and SAS strike at the enemy's rear, and the naval divers keep the sea lanes open, disposing of the mass of ordnance, in Germany the Royal Engineers divers will be with the mechanized armoured brigades whose job it will be to counter an armoured thrust into Western Europe. The Engineer diver is trained in the use of compressed-air equipment, and although they undertake no covert operations, their work certainly is highly dangerous and important.

A river is as great a natural barrier for an army as for anyone else. Obviously helicopters,

Engineers operate world-wide, as shown with the Gurkha engineer diving team.

boats and amphibious vehicles can cross, but the bulk of support equipment needed by an advancing army cannot simply be swum across, for the number of vehicles able to do this is fairly restricted. The main access across a river is by bridge or by a shallow stable area where trucks and heavy vehicles can ford. The other method is by improvised bridging, and the armoured brigades carry bridging units as part of their organization.

Against a powerful enemy thrust, the Engineer diver will be tasked with operating in the fast-flowing rivers of Germany to demolish the bridges and access areas that could be utilized by the enemy. They will be as close to the front line as those fighting to defend it, and will be open to attack from the enemy. They will set traps at key points of embarkation for river crossings and the areas that could be used by the mobile bridge units. The divers in this role will be mobile with trucks and equipment.

French engineer divers aboard a Zodiac prepare to go to a diver training site.

As the enemy advance is halted, and the counter-offensive begins, the combat Engineer diver will move forward in the front line, for the Engineers will be tasked with clearing mine-fields and removing obstructions. They will have to reverse their role, and examine the bridge areas for explosive devices, and aid in the establishment of mobile bridge equipment. Vehicles stuck or trapped in water will have to be recovered and waterways kept clear. Mobility will be a prime consideration, for the thrust cannot stop because of a fast-flowing river or cleverly devised minefield.

* * *

French soldiers, crews of the AMX-30 tanks, watch the parachutes deploy and the troops descend earthwards. A transport aircraft passes over and drops pallets of equipment, which fall unguided under their canopies. The tanks have stopped near a river which needs to be crossed, and they have awaited the arrival of the specialist divers, who will find a crossing location and ensure their safe movement to the opposite

bank. Being dropped by parachute to descend into the water, where they experience no visibility, penetrating cold and a struggle against the current, is part of the French Army diver's job. In the water the paired divers probe the bottom of the river for obstacles, soft mud and enemy anti-tank crossing devices. The report that they make is critical, as the success of the tanks' crossing depends on it.

French Army divers are trained at the Army Diving School (EPAT) of the 4th Regiment, by the staff of the Valbonne, near Lyons. Diving courses last eight weeks, plus the Army's basic parachute course, as all French Army divers are para-qualified. Those who pass the course are qualified as 'Crossing Assistant Specialist' (SAF) and become members of the 4th Regiment. Those who

volunteer begin a course during which the first three weeks are spent on a daily routine of two hours' diving, two hours' sport and four hours of lectures. In the third week the trainees take an elementary Special Development test. This consists of them leaving their equipment of cylinders, weight belt and fins in the gravel at a depth of 8 m (26 ft), returning to the surface, then diving back down to re-equip themselves. The remainder of the course takes place in the river, for the 'crossing' phase of the training, and in the lake where the trainees are taught to use explosives and a wide variety of underwater tools. The last week is devoted to an end of course test.

The culmination of the training course involves a long-distance trek, encompassing a dive to check a river-crossing location, then a seven-hour journey in small boats, followed by a 30 km (18 mile walk). This is accomplished in any weather and with the trainees dressed in wet suits. Whilst waiting for their unit posting,

One diver maintains a watch over the diving boat and equipment, which has attracted the interest of two policemen.

the now qualified divers learn the art of dropping out of helicopters and, depending upon the time of year, they may learn to dive underneath ice. The divers have the benefit of significant pay bonuses to compensate for the unusual tasks and risks they incur, in addition to the additional pay they receive for being parachute qualified.

* * *

The Soviets place a great emphasis on their armoured vehicles being amphibious, and those such as the PT-76 amphibious tank can move from land to water without any special preparation or the need for snorkels. Propulsion is provided when in water by two jets, permanently mounted at the rear of the vehicle. Those that cannot 'swim', can ford, as is the case with the T-62 main battle tank, which when fitted with snorkel equipment can submerge to a depth of 4 m (13 ft), and can be prepared for waterborne operations in about fifteen minutes. This means that the main armoured units and supporting units can cross water barriers without needing bridges or ferrying pontoons.

Not all of those who enter DOSAAF schools are children and young people. At the Tallinn DOSAAF school, training of specialist divers is also undertaken, both for military service and some areas of non-military research work. At Tallinn they expound the virtues of the underwater swimmers, for during the Second World War it was the divers who assisted in laying a pipeline across Lake Ladoga during winter, which provided desperately needed fuel supplies to Leningrad. Having laid it, divers then continued to service it. During the struggle to liberate Kiev, tanks needed to cross the River Dnieper, which meant finding a deep ford. Divers reconnoitred crossing places and supported the action by assisting vehicles that got into difficulty. Today, tanks can ford virtually as deep as required, and this significantly increases the effectiveness of these machines, but they still require the support of engineer combat divers to recce crossing areas, to re-

move obstacles and aid any stricken vehicles.

The Tallinn military diving training course ensures that sufficient divers are trained and available to support the Soviet Armed Forces. Those selected to undertake the specialized course will already be skilled in working with metal and tools. Fitters, mechanics, welders and smithies are prime candidates, as it is quicker to train a diver than to teach a technical skill. During the initial training phase, the students' swimming skills are developed, with prime consideration given to allaying any fear of water. The school does get individuals who, although they feel reasonably at ease on the surface, are terrified of going underwater. In this event there is little that the training staff can do, and they undertake a method of seeking out any such persons as early in the programme as possible. Some students do master the fear, others do not and the latter untrainable conscripts are removed from diver training.

Preceding the armoured units are the specialized engineers who will provide divers to carry out reconnaissance missions of possible crossing locations. The large, fast-flowing rivers of Europe will be a barrier in themselves, and added to that will be the submerged obstructions of mines, barbed wire, and anti-tank devices. The engineers will not have a lot of time to select and prepare a crossing place, as the armoured forces will not want to be held up in a 'stop' position, attracting enemy fire. Of course, NATO engineers will have already 'selected' the areas most likely to be used, and they will be subjected to artillery fire and air strikes. Because of the Soviets' interest in water, and their ability to cross it, their supporting arms include a considerable number of combat divers, able to use the equipment and tackle the task. These divers are drawn not only from the Soviet armed forces, but from their Warsaw Pact allies as well.

Most of the vehicles 'swim' when in water, but the main battle tank continues its journey across the bed of the river. Because it has a depth limit of 4 m (13 ft), the depth soundings

Soviet engineer divers carry out reconnaissance for possible tank-crossing locations.

will have to be accurate. The tanks fitted with snorkels are then driven into the water, to continue along the bottom in the same manner as when on land. Soft silt mud and underwater obstructions are the major causes for concern, but once across, the tanks regain the bank and when possible the crews disassemble the snorkel, remaining battle ready.

Selection and training of underwater swimmers is normally a carefully programmed project, but the Soviets extend the use of underwater breathing equipment to their tank personnel on a wide basis. They can use it either inside the tank or outside, if called to go to the aid of a submerged vehicle.

The following section is taken from Soviet text on the training of their tank personnel. The most significant items of interest are the facts that the entire battalion is trained, and that they use the closed-circuit breathing apparatus. This is more complicated to use than compressed-air systems, and in the UK is reserved for the specialist diver and underwater swimmer.

Frogmen training for tank personnel

During combat operations, tank personnel must overcome various water obstacles either by using special equipment, or by crossing over on the bottom. Numerous exercises and manoeuvres have revealed that the latter method is most suitable. This requires that each member of the crew possesses outstanding specialized training and high moral-political and combat qualities, many of which are developed during frogman training exercises.

Soviet tank crews are taught how to use underwater breathing apparatus.

Prior to being called into the army, Private Shafordiyev did not know how to swim, they taught him how to do so in the unit. But when the time came for him to don a breathing apparatus, he became frightened and was unable to lower himself more than 1 m (39 in) into the water. During training, this soldier constantly removed the rubber facepiece from his head for fear that he would smother. Actually, when an individual experiences fear and his breathing is strained, small amounts of moisture and carbon dioxide may lodge on the absorbent in the regenerative canister, as a result of which the oxygen regeneration process may be inhibited.

During exercises, three other soldiers with the same problem were detected. By the end of the week, there were twelve individuals in the battalion who were unable to perform the submerged exercise using a breathing apparatus. A type of 'deficiency' had developed in the tank crews. In peacetime such a phenomenon can detract from the combat training of the personnel; in wartime it could disrupt fulfilment of a combat task. Obviously, such deficiencies cannot be tolerated.

The sub-unit commander, after studying the psychological qualities of each subordinate, was able to isolate the reason for their failure. During the very next exercise, he said to the solders: 'There is not one among you who is unable to master frogman training. True, some of you require assistance. However I am confident that all of you will soon complete the exercise in a masterful manner.' The tank personnel were encouraged by the officer's words; they became more confident of their abilities.

Exercises were begun in the swimming pool. The soldiers practised diving to shallow depths, other methods for entering the water and moving about under the water with the aid of a rubber breathing tube and carrying a weight – a tank track link or a bag filled with bricks. The students gradually acquired the rudiments of frogman work, recognized their own potential and, even more important, they developed such qualities as bravery and endurance.

During the preparatory period, other important measures were carried out; inspection of the tank personnel by a medical committee, preparation of individual records for frogman training and for operating a tank underwater, checking the proper working order and adjustments of the breathing apparatus and also the swimming jackets and other specialized equipment.

As a rule, the tank personnel study their breathing apparatus in specially equipped classrooms and, during practical exercises, at specialized training locations.

Soldiers should be taught the rules for preparing a breathing apparatus for operation in line with the principle of 'Do as I do' and initially only in stages. Only after this has been done should they be allowed to engage in independent training under an instructor's observation. Initially they should be shown the sequence of operations involved in checking the equipment, and they should be informed regarding the manner in which the apparatus is prepared for use on land and under water. Special attention should be given to selecting the correct facepiece size and checking it for hermetic tightness. Thereafter they should be shown the various positions for the respirator; 'march', 'at the ready' and 'combat', for use on the ground outside a tank, inside a tank and under the water.

It is important for the tank personnel to study well the sequence to be followed in all operations, to constantly monitor the proper positioning of the mouthpiece and the nose clamp and to know how to actuate the starting briquette.

Certainly, there is nothing new here. Never-theless the principal statutes of frogman training bear mentioning once again and emphasis should be placed on ensuring that the requirements of all of the instructions and rules are firmly and strictly observed. True, the learning documents at times furnish only general recommendations, with the details having to be procured during actual practice.

When wearing a breathing apparatus, one must observe a strict breathing regime; inhaling and exhaling must be deeper and the frequency of breathing must be somewhat less than under ordinary circumstances. Upon entering the water, one should raise the respirator with one hand to prevent it from becoming wet. Once the water rises to chest level, one should exhale fully, holding the breath and quickly submerge, releasing the respirator as one does so. The fact of the matter is that if the respirator is submerged coincidental with inhaling, the water will squeeze the respiratory bag such that it will be impossible to fill it with oxygen (the lungs will be unable to overcome the water pressure). As a result, the exhaled air, in addition to passing through the regeneration cartridge, will also pass through (a portion of the exhaled air) the area under the facepiece and directly into the water. The 'scouring' of the oxygen will have a very adverse effect on the well-being of the student and as a rule he will be unable to complete the exercise.

In conclusion it should be noted that frogman training personnel requires special attention. Success in the training of subordinates is usually achieved by those commanders who organize and conduct their exercises in a creative manner and whose students perform their duties in an efficient and irreproachable manner, observing all safety rules.

Yet again this serves to show the wide range of personnel in the Soviet and Warsaw Pact forces who are trained and skilled to some degree in underwater swimming.

Chapter 11
The infiltration of assault swimmers

Numerous options are available for the infiltration of assault swimmers. These range from submarines, surface ships and boats, to helicopters and fixed-wing aircraft. All can play an important role in providing a flexible mode of delivery, and the method chosen will depend on a number of factors, as covert operations re-

quire teams to enter enemy territory unseen, to avoid compromising an operation.

Parachuting

All special forces troops are trained in the art of parachuting, the most common method being the static-line drop. This is where the parachutist hooks up a line from his main parachute to a fixed point in the aircraft, so that when he jumps, the line pays out behind him,

Combat swimmers stand with parachute static lines clipped on, ready to make a 'wet' parachute drop.

Above Special Boat Squadron swimmers undertake 'wet' parachute drop from a Hercules C130.

Right Free-fall parachuting provides greater accuracy.

craft to drop back down to a safe level again.

Dropping men and equipment into the sea is a difficult task, for both need to be close together. On land, if a team is spread out they can walk to collect their equipment and assemble, but in the sea, waves, tides and current all create problems, a long swim may ensue, and packages are very difficult to move in water.

The Special Boat Squadron deploys teams into a target area using the static-line method of parachuting, although they use HALO and HAHO parachuting techniques for certain operations. They are skilled in dropping into the water, and on to land.

Most mechanical items do not react well

pulling the canopy out of its bag, allowing it to deploy automatically. If the main canopy should have a malfunction, the parachutist can use his emergency parachute, carried on the front of his body, which is deployed manually.

The advantages of the static-line method is that it is well proven, easy to learn and relatively safe. The men can carry considerable equipment loads, and today, using steerable canopies, land close to the target. The normal drop height with this method of parachuting is in the 150 to 600 m (490–1,970 ft) height range. It is the best method for undertaking 'wet' drops, and combined with the use of the 6.7 m (22 ft) steerable canopy, can provide great accuracy when attempting to land close to stores or to a vessel waiting in the water. The transport aircraft, which in the West would probably be a Hercules C-130 and in the East an An-12 Cub, would, on a covert mission, fly low to avoid radar detection, lifting up for the parachute drop at the last moment. At the minimum altitude, the men and equipment will disgorge themselves rapidly, to allow the air-with water, and in consequence the SBS allow a fifty per cent 'fudge factor', which means that they expect or plan for a fifty per cent failure of equipment. The result is that an operational team will require a considerable payload of stores to support their operation. The failure of equipment, combined with the possible loss of stores packages dropped into the sea, all unite to create problems which could result in an operation failing. With the swimmers go their canoes and Gemini or Zodiac inflatable boats. They can either be dropped in containers, which means the men have to swim them to a safe area on land or to a vessel, where they can be assembled; or they can be parachuted assembled, rafted on pallets, into the sea. The swimmers can then swim to join them then cut away the pallets, which sink, allowing them to paddle their canoes away or start the outboard engines, and power their inflatable boats away.

The swimmers themselves will be dressed in underwater swimming dry suits. A heavy duty suit is used for the cold north, with the option of a lightweight one for warm water areas. They are one piece, flexible rubber suits, which seal at the neck and wrists. Entry is through the rear, which zips closed with a waterproof zip. The swimmers' fins are stowed in their parachute harnesses, and can be put on once in the water, or during the descent. The men's Bergens are sealed in waterproof bags, which keeps them dry and provides buoyancy. They will carry the vital equipment needed once on the operation, including the closed-circuit underwater breathing apparatus.

Two points of note should be made here. Swimmers on operations do not normally wear wet suits, although they are commonly used when training in wet parachuting and small boat work, normally in warm water. Nor do swimmers wear underwater breathing apparatus (UBA) when parachuting, not only because the webbing straps of the parachute harness would not allow the apparatus to function until the parachute had been disposed of, but also because the bulk of the UBA set on the swimmer's front could jeopardize the reserve

parachute's function. Swimmers use the parachute to enter an area near a target, and would be unlikely to envisage a situation where they would need to enter the water and descend immediately below the surface to swim away to a target, for if dropped that close to the target, they would certainly be compromised. In addition, the amount of equipment required, the 'fudge factor', and the possibility of extreme weather conditions, would make it impracticable. So the swimmers are dropped, with their equipment, well clear of the final target

Equipment is rafted for a parachute drop into the sea.

Whilst most wet parachute drops require dry diving suits, SEALs parachuting into the Pacific are dressed for the occasion.

area, and they then use their specialist skills of movement over land or by water along the coastline to an area from which they can carry out the mission.

For one particular SBS section dropping through the night sky, the ground loomed below and as they landed a great deal of confusion greeted them, for they had landed in an enemy camp. Whilst the enemy gathered itself, the SBS men made good their escape and found a stream which they followed for about an hour, only to run into an ambush by an enemy patrol. In this case, the drop of the SBS men into an

'enemy' camp had been intentional, although neither side had been pre-warned. It was done as a test to assess the reactions of both groups when presented with the problem, for in war it could very well happen.

Apart from parachuting into the sea, close to the land or into a fjord, swimmers could easily drop into a lake, possibly miles inland, where they could make use of any small islands and the normally abundant vegetation found near larger areas of water. The swimmers on this type of operation would probably be from the Special Air Service boat troop, and they would almost certainly use high altitude free fall methods. The High Altitude Low Opening (HALO) technique requires the parachutist to depart the aircraft at an altitude of some

7,500 m (24,600 ft) whilst breathing oxygen, and to track across the sky in the free fall position, gaining ground distance whilst descending. When the parachutist reaches the canopy deployment altitude, the parachute can be opened manually or automatically, to complete the descent in the conventional manner. The amount of equipment that can be carried by the individual is very limited, especially if underwater breathing apparatus is added. A team can jump with a separate stores container, however, which means the men have to track it across the sky then, near the canopy deployment altitude, separate and follow it down to the ground. This method is acceptable on land, but it would require considerable training to undertake such a drop into the sea.

High Altitude High Opening (HAHO) is the other specialist techniqe. This again requires the parachutist to depart the aircraft at high altitude, breathing oxygen, but differs from HALO in that the parachutist departs the aircraft, stabilizes in the free fall mode, then deploys his canopy. This would be a ram air wing, which permits a great deal of control and which when used by skilful operators, can fly a man across the sky, covering a considerable ground distance. Again, this method limits the amount of equipment the individual can carry, and would require a separate container drop, or a rendezvous at a pre-sited stores cache.

The full viability of free fall parachuting in the military context is much argued about. The SAS and SBS train and specialize in the high altitude free fall and static-line parachute, and would assess a combat situation before deciding upon a particular method to be used.

Special Air Service boat troop swimmers are trained in the use of closed-circuit underwater breathing apparatus by the Royal Navy, as the Regiment does not have the necessary facilities or supervisor instructors within its establishment. Initial diving training is undertaken with the Royal Engineers, and the SAS men then move on to the oxygen rebreathing sets to allow a clandestine mode of underwater swimming. The SAS calls on the services of the Royal Navy's diving branch when they have a 'wet' operation. The Navy's man, a Chief Petty Officer, is fully conversant with diving, the rules and equipment. In one instance, however, when the dedicated 'Chief' was collected by some unidentified members of the SAS Regiment and whisked off to an unknown airfield, guided on to an aircraft, set down amidst rubber-suited bodies and strapped in, it was not, for him, normal. This became even more apparent when, after a period of time in the air, the men stood up, faced towards the back of the aircraft and watched the tail door open. They then moved back and out of the aircraft, leaving only the straps of their static lines as evidence of their having been there. The Chief could only observe his 'responsiblity' floating down to the sea below, under the dark mushroom canopies of their parachutes. This incident actually happened: the poor Chief was returned to the airfield and eventually to Portsmouth, not knowing where his 'diving' team was. Much amusement was later made of the fact that it had been indicated to the Chief that he might be seconded to the SAS and have to undertake the selection course...

The use of either high altitude parachuting or low static-line techniques, with precision landing, could become a viable option if entering a NATO country such as Norway. Stores could be pre-cached near a coastline, in a known area, so that an operation would be a matter of infiltrating swimmers on to land, complete with personal Bergens and weapons, who could then RV at the cache and prepare for their mission. In the case of Norway, however, special problems arise with stores left in pre-determined caches, especially in winter, for it would be difficult to find stores buried underground when they are covered with deep snow.

Aircraft capable of transporting parachutist/swimmers are numerous both in the NATO alliance and the Warsaw Pact, the most common being the C-130 Hercules and An-12 which both have aircrews conversant with the needs of the Special Forces. For air drops, however, there has been increasing expansion

in the use of helicopters. Experience in Afghanistan and the Falklands has shown that, even though they have noisy engines, they are able to fly very low and fast, using the cover of undulating terrain to enter enemy territory and deposit teams. At night, helicopter aircrews can use passive night-vision equipment to enable them to undertake tasks that normally would only be envisaged during daylight. The only really dangerous conditions are in snow white-outs, when the crew cannot see anything and have to rely totally on instruments. Helicopters are improving in terms of survivability and endurance, and are a viable option for delivering swimmers to a land or water rendezvous, by jumping from low altitude, abseiling or parachuting. Modern helicopters can carry ever-increasing quantities of stores as well.

The parachutist dropping into water has a number of important factors to consider. He does not want his presence to be indicated to searching enemy vessels and aircraft, and he must obviously take account of sea and wind conditions. Criteria for an operational drop will be different to those on a training exercise, but there are limits. One problem a parachutist dropping into the sea encounters is that of judging his height, for over land he may be able to see things below which he can relate to in terms of height, but the open sea, in either daylight or shimmering in the moonlight, is a different proposition. Then, once the swimmer enters the water he is followed by the shrouds and canopy, which, if they fall on top of him can become at least a nuisance, and at worst, fatal. One swimmer descending into the water at night thought he was lower than he was and released himself from the harness, so allowing the canopy to be carried clear of him. He had totally misjudged the height and fell awkwardly into the sea, and was killed.

Above left SBS team members in a Hercules C130 travel to the drop zone.

Left SBS teams can be dropped off with their equipment by helicopter.

An aid to the parachutist at night is the fact that the waterproofed Bergen which hangs below him hits the water first, thus indicating a reasonable distance to drop if he releases himself from the harness.

Rendezvousing with a submarine at sea is a fast method of getting a team to a covert destination if a target zone air drop is impracticable. A pre-determined RV is decided upon between the submarine and the aircraft, the factors of current and wind speed and direction being accounted for. The aircraft will travel to the drop zone and make contact with the submerged boat, whose captain will have to determine whether to remain submerged, or surface to take the swimmers aboard. The submarine's fin makes a large splash on a radar scanner, including those of anti-ship aircraft, and if the captain feels that the pick up could be compromised he will remain submerged. If it is safe, he will surface and the fin will provide a good marker for the drop aircraft. The boat can also discharge a smoke flare to aid identification, and at night illuminating flares could also be used, not only for the aircraft to align on, but for the swimmer/parachutists to steer towards.

With the boat on the surface, and virtually stopped, the only forward movement being that needed to keep some form of headway, the swimmers will be dropped so that they can make use of their steerable parachutes to control their descent to land as close as possible to the submarine. The separate stores containers cannot be steered, and so the skill of the aircrew is needed to drop them at the best position to ensure that they enter the water close to the boat. Members of the submarine's crew, conversant with covert swimmer operations, are able to assist from the deck in getting both men and equipment aboard and stowed below as quickly as possible. It is possible that the section's Gemini inflatables or canoes will be dropped ready to use; if they are, the teams can get aboard and manoeuvre the stores to the submarine more quickly. Once aboard the Geminis can be deflated, and boat and engine either put below or stored in the casing deck

156

containers, while canoes can be stored below without having to be dismantled.

It is much more difficult for a section to join a submerged submarine. Again radio contact is made between the boat and the aircraft, and again flares can be used to pin-point the boat's position. The swimmer/parachutists are then dropped upstream of the submarine, which will be at periscope depth.

Once the swimmers are in the water, they will discard their parachutes and fit their fins. Any stores containers which have been dropped are gathered together, then the men swim at intervals along a rope connecting them, until it is stretched out. The two outside swimmers each carry an underwater transponder beacon which emits a signal through the water. Lowered deeper into the water, the transponders reply to a signal received from the submarine's transducer, which the submarine 'picks up' on its sonar screen, and the positions are plotted. With the two beacons transmitting, the Captain of the boat is able to steer a course to the mid-point of the swimmers' rope.

The swimmers strung out on the line will move up and down in the swell, often not able to see each other let alone the periscope until it is very close. The submarine is able to move ahead slowly, keeping the two beacon signals either side of centre. The periscope will then catch the rope, hopefully at mid-point, and pull the swimmers into line behind it. The swimmers' leader will inform the Captain via the underwater communications that they have been snagged – as will the beacons, which should be together, astern of the boat. The sumbarine will then stop and prepare to take aboard the swimmers, who, if they have not already done so, will put on their UBAs and prepare to dive down to the boat.

The first two swimmers will go down, following the periscope and fin to the special stowage boxes between the pressure hull and the deck casing. Whilst one opens these, the other will release a rope with a buoy on the end. Returning to the surface, they and the other swimmers will attach their containers to the line, and reduce their buoyancy, allowing them to sink to the casing where they can be stored in stowage boxes. Then, depending upon the size of the escape chamber, from two to five swimmers will enter and close the outer door. The water is then vented out, allowing the inside door to open, and enabling the swimmers to enter the submarine. The inner door is closed and sealed again, then pressurized to equal the depth of water, whereupon the next group of swimmers will follow the same procedure, until all are aboard, and the submarine can dive deeper and proceed upon its course.

Submarines

Both conventional and nuclear-powered submarines are used for clandestine underwater swimming operations, the latter having the disadvantages of being comparatively noisy and unable to 'bottom out'. This is a manoeuvre in which the submarine moves into shallow water and then sits on the sea-bed to allow swimmers to exit and re-enter, or to deploy swimmer delivery vehicles, which the larger types of submarine may carry to a target. Nuclear-powered submarines have cooling-water intakes for their reactors, set in the bottom of the hull, and so require a certain amount of clear water below them. On the advantage side, the nuclear boat is faster, and has more room for the additional people and stores. During the Falklands' conflict, SAS and SBS swimmers were dropped from Hercules aircraft to rendezvous with submarines, which then carried them to their drop-off areas at sea. All exits from submarines in the Falklands' operations were done whilst the boats were on the surface, and no underwater swimmer lock-outs were undertaken. Geminis and canoes were used by swimmers from both SBS and SAS, which allowed the teams to carry the equipment and stores needed to survive and fight in the extreme conditions. There was no need for underwater covert attacks from a submerged submarine, as both South Georgia and the Falklands had vast expanses of exposed

HMS *Osiris*, like her sister *Onyx*, is an 'Oberon' class patrol submarine, providing the principal submarine delivery units for SBS swimmer teams.

coastline which enabled the swimmers to get ashore by more conventional means, along with the additional 'fudge factor' stores.

HMS *Onyx* carried out a number of covert operations in the Falklands' conflict. Carrying teams of the SBS, she moved in close to land at night, then surfaced to deploy the Gemini inflatable boats, which carried the special forces troops ashore, leaving the submarine free to move back out to sea again. There are numerous dangers in such operations for any submarine, and *Onyx* sustained damage to one of her torpedo tubes containing a live torpedo. As a result she had to return to the UK for repairs. When one considers the size of a submarine such as *Onyx*, whose crew of seventy are all housed in extremely cramped conditions, the addition of SBS or SAS swimmer teams, often in large numbers, adds considerably to the discomfort; the inside of a conventional submarine gets very hot and clammy, especially with additional men drawing on the air conditioning. 'Home' for the swimmer teams is in the spare torpedo stowage area, which they share with rubber boats, outboard engines, canoes and the mass of other specialist equipment. There are no bunks for them.

Because of the 'fudge factor', it is desirable for submarine swimmer operations to be prepared in a dock, harbour or sheltered water, where all equipment can be checked and stowed prior to the operation's commencement, thus giving more flexibility to the team in the target area. Canoes and Gemini inflatable boats can be stowed below decks or in the stowage boxes under the casing. Canoes carried inside the pressure hull can be assembled ready for use, but if stowed collapsed, they will be in three separate bags. British submariners are very familiar with the needs of both the SBS and SAS, and are extremely efficient at manhandling the equipment both out on to the deck and into the water, as their counterparts in the US and Soviet navies are with the requirements of their own special forces. Canoes and Geminis can be deployed in one of two ways, the first requiring the boats to be launched into the water, with the swimmers climbing down into them. The other method is to leave the canoes or boats on the submarine's deck with the team aboard, whereupon the submarine will sink slowly down, allowing the boats to float and move clear. The latter is quicker and is the method

favoured, especially when the Captain does not want to keep his submarine on the surface longer than necessary. Recovery of either craft will be by bringing them alongside, so that the men can clamber up on to the casing, while the submarine's crew drags the boats up to the deck and stows them away.

To deliver its cargo of specialist troops, the submarine will sail to the predetermined 'drop off' area, where it will either surface to dispatch its teams, or do so while submerged. For a covert operation that requires the submarine to remain submerged, the boat will move to a position in which to bottom out. Once in position, two swimmers will enter the escape chamber and flood it to gain access to the water outside. These men are known as the 'casing divers', and their job is to remain in the lurking area, where they will firstly send a buoy attached to a line to the surface, the line running close to the exit hatch of the escape chamber. The casing divers will then remove the boats and stores from the storage boxes under the casing deck and inflate them, sending them to the surface attached to the rope.

On the surface the inflated craft, with their waterproofed outboard engines, are ready for the stores to be put aboard. The number of boats used will obviously depend upon the numbers in the teams on a given operation. Once the boats are on the surface and ready, the casing divers inform the teams inside. The first group enters the escape chamber, and begins to equalize to the surrounding pressure. Outside the two divers stand by the hatch with the rope ready for the swimmers. As the hatch begins to open, the divers assist with pulling it open, allowing the swimmers to emerge, wearing limited-endurance underwater breathing sets. They are handed the rope by the divers, so that they can follow it to the surface.

The breathing sets they use for this operation have only a few minutes duration and so speed, combined with safety, is essential. The first swimmers reaching the surface will get aboard the inflatables and prepare the outboard engines. Each man will be wearing his combat

Above Two SBS swimmers in the lock out chamber of a submarine.

Above far left SBS canoe team depart from a surfaced submarine with the aid of the crew.

Above left Inflatable boats are placed on the deck of a surfaced submarine and when the swimmers are aboard the submarine submerges leaving the boat to move away.

Left With boats stowed, the swimmers go below to allow the submarine to submerge.

suit, encased in an underwater dry swim suit. The breathing sets would be of little use on an operation and would be discarded, although on an exercise they would be salvaged. The remaining swimmers then exit the submarine and are guided to the surface where, once they are all aboard, they depart, leaving the casing divers to secure the line and hatches. The casing divers will have spent a considerable time in the water and will wear a warmer Uni suit (described later), which offers much greater protection than the standard dry suit. The hatches secured and the line disposed of, the divers re-enter the submarine to await the recovery of the swimmer teams at a pre-determined time. For them, whilst the submarine moves clear of the rendezvous, it is a time to rest.

At the pre-arranged time the swimmers will move out to sea aboard their boats, and at the rendezvous lower a transponder or a bongle (a hollow tube in which two balls knock together, emitting enough sound to be heard by the submarine) into the water. The submarine will pick up the signal on its sonar, and move in to pick up. With just the periscope up, the Captain may not be able to see the small inflatable, but he will certainly be able to search for any other vessels, especially enemy ones which could cause problems. At the rendezvous, the swimmers will be able to converse with the submarine's Captain, and when the latter is satisfied that the re-entry can begin, he will give the okay to the two casing divers, who will be ready to enter the escape chamber. Once locked out, they will again dispatch to the surface a line with a buoy attached. They can then take short-duration underwater breathing sets up for those who need them. The boats and stores are recovered by deflating them and allowing them to sink down to the submarine's deck. Whilst the casing divers stow the equipment away, the first group of swimmers enter the chamber, and re-enter the submarine.

This process continues until all of the swimmers are aboard, then once the equipment is stowed and secured, the casing divers re-enter. If at any point during the recovery the Captain or Commander of the swimmer groups feels that the rendezvous could be compromised, the swimmers are recovered and their boats and stores discarded after they have been suitably damaged to ensure that they sink. It is also possible for swimmers in inflatables or canoes, rendezvousing with a submerged submarine in an area where they could be compromised, to be towed away from the area and recovered in a safer location.

The Dutch SBS may operate from British submarines, but if they use their own boats and combine with Belgian commando combat swimmers, they will use the torpedo tubes to exit and re-enter the submarine, and to transport their equipment. The Russians and Warsaw Pact combat swimmers utilize their submarines' torpedo tubes for this purpose, too.

Rather than commit a large submarine to a covert operations role, when it could be more usefully employed in its conventional role of hunter killer, a small specialized submarine can be a more suitable alternative. The Piranha is one such concept, designed specially for the role of covert missions and developed by the UK shipbuilders Vickers. Able to carry a team of ten special forces troops, it can deliver them to a target area, where they can disembark whilst the submarine is on the surface, or they can be locked out using the methods already described, two swimmers at a time. A pair of two-man swimmer delivery vehicles can be carried, one either side of the hull, or it could be feasible to carry two subskimmer craft in special garages. These are able to carry more swimmers, and extend the operational range of the Piranha. If an operation were a seaborne swimmer raid against a harbour, the SDVs would be replaced by six high-capacity bottom-laid mines; then, whilst the swimmers undertook a limpet raid, the Piranha could lay the mines.

The relatively small length of the vessel, at 26.6 m (87.3 ft), makes it ideal for its role in special operations, as it is able to penetrate into shallower water with a low risk of detection. Even when on the surface, its fin is extremely small when compared with its larger sisters. The vessel's range is very good – a transit range of 1,800 nautical miles on continuous snort, an operational radius of 800 nautical miles, and a range of seventy nautical miles at four knots completely submerged. Stores carried on board allow the seven-men crew and ten special forces troops to remain on patrol for twelve days.

'Piranha' carries a range of equipment to aid operations, including passive sonar, noise-monitoring sonar, a radar warning receiver, and both attack and search periscopes. These are combined with transceivers and antennae to communicate in the HF and UHF bands.

The United States of America has had the capability of delivering more than 60 combat swimmers in covert amphibious operations, in

the form of the submarine USS *Grayback*. Although now ending her active life, her role has been the basis of further development in special forces submarines. The formar Polaris missile submarines USS *Sam Houston* and USS *John Marshall* have been converted for special operations, each able to carry 65 combat swimmers and one swimmer delivery vehicle, vital to the future of underwater operations. The adaption for combat swimmer operations involves the addition of dry deck shelters (DDS), which comprise three sections. Two are cylindrical and link the DDS to the submarine's escape hatch and allow swimmer decompression, whilst the third section, also cylindrical, houses the SDV. The larger chamber also means that a

Above 'Piranha', with a swimmer delivery vehicle carried on the side.

Below The control room of Piranha.

Top A modified Soviet 'Yankee' class submarine. The large hangar to the rear of the fin is thought to house minisubs for covert missions.

Above The might of the US Navy's nuclear-powered submarine force will provide an advanced combat swimmer and swimmer delivery vehicle conversion system.

large lock-out of swimmers can be undertaken in one go.

It had been planned to convert the *Sam Houston* and *John Marshall* to carry two DDSs, but due to unforeseen problems this was not done, and they come to the end of their active life in the early 1990s. Therefore the future of submarine support may depend on the conversion of six long-hulled 'Sturgeon' class attack submarines, each to carry a single DDS. The attack submarine USS *Cavalla* has already been modified for a special forces role, but at present it means that there are three converted submarines and only two shelters, with a third being fabricated.

If only six submarines are converted, it does limit the operational capabilities of the

The SBS still use the famous Klepper canoe for covert infiltration.

SEALs, whose complement is rapidly expanding.

Raiding craft

The SBS and SAS covert swimmers have a diverse range of craft available to them, apart from the larger power vessels and aircraft. The traditional Klepper canoe used by both units has its origins in the Second World War, and is a highly versatile swimmer platform. Carrying two men, it has a low silhouette, a useful requirement considering today's radar systems. It can be used at sea and in shallow inland rivers, is stable and can carry a payload of some 450 kg (1,000 lb). It can be stripped down for transportation in three separate bags, and when assembled, can be carried overland by two men. It can be dropped from an aircraft, assembled on a raft or bagged. In short it is a flexible and silent vehicle. On an operation the

craft can be paddled with double paddles, or by singles when a very low profile is needed. Ashore, the swimmers can hide it, by tipping it on its side, allowing it to fill with water, and then leaving it on the bottom, to be recovered when needed to carry its team away.

In the Falklands, SAS boat troop teams were deposited by helicopter along with their canoes, which they assembled and carried down to the beach of a deserted island. They paddled across a channel to land on Pebble Island, where they could have sunk the craft or carried them into the undergrowth to camouflage them in hides, allowing the teams to move off to undertake their intelligence-gathering operations. When the mission was accomplished, the men moved out of the OP, collected their canoes and paddled back to the small island to be recovered by helicopter. The canoeists were able to provide valuable in-

Left The Klepper frame, and with its skin on. The canoe is collapsible and can be stowed in bags for transportation or parachute drops.

Below Danish Sovaerns Fromandskorps SBS canoe teams infiltrate ashore.

telligence to the planners, and also able to take part in an attack against an Argentinian airfield.

Transportation by Rigid Raiders of the Commandos raiding squadrons is another possibility. Canoes can be laid across the beam, their crews crouching in the Raider, which will use its high speed and the cover of darkness to get the canoe team closer to their target. For the swimmers, the canoe provides a base, as well as a shelter in extreme conditions. The craft can be laid up in shallow water, hidden in overhanging undergrowth or rocks, allowing the team to remain in it; although extremely cramped, it does afford some protection.

All manner of weapons can be carried and fired from the Klepper canoe, from the 9 mm automatic pistol, through the General Purpose Machine-Gun to the LAW disposable rocket launcher. Even mortars can be fired from the canoe with, of course, much modification because of the downward kick when firing the weapon. Radios, food, personal equipment, underwater swimming apparatus and mines are all part of the diverse payload that can be carried by the two-man team. Although the canoe is slow moving when compared with the raiding craft and Geminis, it does not have the 'fudge factor' of engine failure. Used in numbers, canoes can be rafted together to allow the swimmers to enter the water more easily. To accomplish this, the canoes move alongside each other to create a stable platform and the number twos assist the number ones to put on their breathing sets, whilst at the same time the number twos maintain the crafts' position. The swimmers dressed and equipped for the water ease out of their cockpits and move across the bows to enter the water. The swimmers, in pairs, link their buddy lines and vent their suits. They then move alongside the canoes where the number twos hand them the stores, and as the swimmers move away, one of the remaining canoeists informs the HQ by radio that the raid is under way.

The weather is a major factor in all small boat operations, but as one team found in Nor-thern Norway, the water is often warmer than the land. Having been deposited at sea from a surfaced submarine, the canoeists made for a rendezvous on land. Dressed in combat kit, with the underwater apparatus and suits stowed in their canoe, they arrived at the pre-arranged location and moved into hides. When they came to preparing their underwater equipment, the suits were found to be frozen solid with the residue of dampness from the surrounding atmosphere. To defrost them, the men had to immerse their suits in the water; after a period of time the higher temperature of the water, compared with that of the ground and air, defrosted them. However, not all canoe operations are undertaken in the frozen north, and whereas cold is one enemy, the sea holds others.

I can recall one event during canoe training in the seas around Southern Arabia. 'Spud' Murphy in the aft seat of the canoe paddled fast to keep it straight in the surf as we approached the beach. At the right time I had to clamber out and maintain the boat's momentum up on to the beach, allowing Spud to get out, where we then lifted the canoe up and carried it clear of the water. We were taking part in an exercise in launching, landing and capsize drills, the latter being given an added impetus as the water was shark-infested. In fact, part of the diving training was the inspection of the shark net surrounding the safe swimming area.

We launched the canoe yet again and paddled clear of the surf and breaking waves to move out to sea. It does not take long to travel a considerable distance with both canoeists paddling in co-ordination, and we were soon well out from the shore. We were concentrating on a unified powerful stroke, the canvas-skinned canoe flexing under the contrasting pressures.

The black shape which rose out of the sea, as if in slow motion, caught both of us by surprise. Leaving a trail of foam, it continued up over the bow of our craft to dive into the sea on the other side. Was it a dolphin or a 'large fish'? We did not know, for it happened so quickly, there one moment and gone the next. In unison

Above Danish SBS semi-rigid inflatable drops combat swimmers into the water.

Above left Zodiac can provide a mobile weapon platform in support of amphibious operations.

Left Carrying a number of troops, the Zodiac is a flexible special forces craft.

our paddle blades dug into the water and slewed the canoe round, as our heads screwed in every direction to see if the monster would again rise from the sea. It did not, and no sighting was made. We paddled fast for the distant shore-line, not in panic, but for fear of the fact that if the creature decided to play, our flimsy craft might not last very long. For the surface swimmer, sharks are a constant source of terror, for they are an efficient machine in water, while man is not. We never saw the creature again, but it was big, equal to the length of our two seater canoe, and it could certainly jump well clear of the water.

Rubber inflatable boats such as Geminis and Zodiacs also offer a flexible platform for assault swimmers, as they have a relatively low profile, while the larger models can carry a considerable payload. Powered by a range of outboard engines, they have a speed and range that is acceptable, and which can be extended by additional fuel stocks. They do have two disadvantages, one being the noise, and the other the 'fudge factor', the susceptibility of the outboard engines to mechanical failure. Inflatables can be paddled or rowed, but are then at a disadvantage when compared with a canoe, because they are larger and slower. They can, however, be rafted up in the water to provide a stable platform from which to work, and can, as described earlier, be dropped by parachute, with outboard engines fitted and all equipment stowed inside. When they are dropped into the sea on pallets, the swimmers can use their own steerable parachute canopies to get close to the boats, then once aboard cut the pallets' securing straps to let the boats float clear, thus allowing a rapid deployment of team into enemy territory.

Ashore, the boat can be deflated and packed into bags, and along with the outboard engines, be manpacked overland to a rendezvous or safe location. Provided they are sealed into waterproofed bags, the engines can be buried along with the boat and other equipment in caches, for retrieval after an operation. On one SBS raid on the Falklands two 'fudge factor' 35 hp outboard engines were sealed in bags and buried in the sand for three weeks. The team recovered and fitted them to a Gemini to make their departure, and they started on the first attempt.

On another occasion, a section was assembling an inflatable at sea, in reasonably shallow water off the UK, when they dropped an engine. One of the swimmers put on his UBA and, taking a rope, dived down to the sea bed. Finding the engine he tied the rope to it, whereupon it was recovered to the surface. In place on the stern of the Gemini and drained of water, the engine fired third time, to run faultlessly for the remainder of the operation.

Outboard engines which, although waterproofed, are not sealed, are one of the many problems encountered by all amphibious units. Amidst the ever-continuing trials run by the SBS it is the 'Mariner' engine that has been found to best meet their requirements. In the Falklands, the SAS used a range of Johnson engines, and experienced considerable problems with them, to the extent of total failure which allowed teams to drift into the open South Atlantic. It is of interest to note that, whilst the SBS are primarily dedicated to covert amphibious operations, the SAS use the amphibious capability more for 'getting from A to B', and as such do not appear to have the same testing and experimental commitment of the SBS. Current thinking regarding outboard engines is that a smaller 20 hp model is preferable to one of 40 hp, since two can be fitted to a Gemini, providing the same total output, but if one fails the boat can be powered on the remaining engine, though not quickly. Also, it is easier to manpack the smaller engines than the big one.

Cold and moisture are two of the outboard engine's worst adversaries. One team who had

come ashore by Gemini, hid both boat and outboard engine. When they arrived back after the operation, they recovered both, but found that moisture inside the engine had frozen, rendering it inoperable. The team had to strip down the engine, remove the ice, then reassemble it, before it could be fitted to the inflatable to power them away.

The Dell Quay Dory 17 Rigid Raiding craft, conceived in 1970, can, as described earlier, carry canoes, their teams and stores to a drop-off point. It can also be used to infiltrate special forces troops, and it was these craft manned by the Royal Marines Raiding Squadron that inserted members of the SBS and SAS into the Falkland Islands.

Within its length of 5.20 m (17 ft) and beam of 2.20 m (7 ft) it can carry ten persons and 900 kg (2,000 lb) of equipment. It is an excellent surf and shallow-water boat, and being of foam-filled construction, is unsinkable, even when swamped with water. Its powerful 140 hp outboard engine can power the craft at over 20 knots when fully laden, whilst with a light load it can reach speeds of up to 35 knots. Because of the size and low profile of the craft, it can be used as a fire support vessel, able to carry a wide range of weapons.

Recent developments in hovercraft technology have enhanced their operational capability, and in a recent display at Portsmouth a new military model was found to be highly manoeuvrable, and possibly more important, extremely quiet. The British Hovercraft Corporation probably leads the world in air cushion technology, and although the Royal Navy has disbanded its hovercraft unit, the potential uses of these craft in amphibious operations are numerous.

The AP 1.88 is very flexible and could carry up to 100 troops or twelve tons of equipment. In support of swimmer assault, the half well deck variant could carry forty troops and a range of small raiding craft, whether Dorys, inflatables, canoes or subskimmers, in the well deck area. Another advantage of the hovercraft is its ability to provide supporting firepower in the form of heavy machine-guns or missiles. They can extract troops by mounting a beach, even if mined, and are not affected by any underwater obstructions. Whether a hovercraft would deliver its swimmers on to a beach, with their stores, or lie offshore, allowing the small raiding craft to depart on the raid, would depend upon the particular operation, but the hovercraft certainly offers a flexible command and assault base.

SEAL teams use equipment designed originally for other purposes than special forces' operations. The Inflatable Boat Small (IBS) is no exception, and was originally designed by the US Navy as an emergency lifeboat for sea-going vessels, before being procured by the SEALs for use in a variety of ways. It can be paddled, or fitted with an outboard engine, and rigged with a parachute allowing it to be dropped from an aircraft in para-amphibious operations. It is ideally suited for launch and recovery from the deck of a submarine, whether surfaced or submerged. Carrying seven men, it also has room for 450 kg (1,000 lbs) of equipment.

Larger craft came into the scene during the Vietnam war, when UDT and SEAL team operations were expanded. The Landing Craft Personnel Launch (LCPL) has a length of 11 m (36 ft) and is powered by a 300 hp Gray Marine diesel engine, which produces a speed of some seventeen knots. The Boston Whaler is also used for insertion and extraction, and can be fitted with weapons capable of giving fire support. Its size, of 5 m (16 ft) length and 1.8 m (6 ft) beam combine with the shallow 60 cm (2 ft) draught to make it ideal for riverine operations. It can be powered by either 40 or 80 hp outboard engines.

'Stab' is larger than the Boston Whaler, but is used in the same role. With its 8 m (26 ft) length it provides a greater firepower capability, and it is powered by two 325 hp engines which produce a speed of 45 knots. The Medium SEAL Support Craft (MSSC) has the ability to carry a SEAL platoon. Its length of 11 m (36 ft) requires two 325 hp engines to deliver a speed of thirty knots. It carries heavy machine-gun fire support.

The PTF is also used in special operations for insertion and extraction of SEAL teams. It has heavy armament and is used as a fire support craft in shallow waters. Its 29 m (95 ft) hull is powered by a 6,200 hp engine, which produces a speed of 45 knots.

New to the SEALs inventory is the Seafox, another 11 m (36 ft) high speed, low profile craft developed for special warfare operations. It carries a formidable range of weaponry in the form of .50 cal and M60 .30 machine-guns and a Mark 19 Mod 3 40 mm Automatic Grenade Launcher. This craft, with the others available, ensures good support for SEAL teams' operations.

The enhanced survivability of modern tactical helicopters has made them very acceptable for clandestine operations, both for infiltration and extraction. As well as fast boats for drop off and pick up, the SEAL team swimmers also use the helicopter. A metal bar is rigged inside the aircraft in such a way that it protrudes from the aircraft's door for about three feet. An aluminium-runged wire-rope ladder is also rigged in the aircraft door, for use in the pick up. The swimmers will wear a wet suit, face mask, lifejacket and fins, and will carry a knife and flare. As the aircraft approaches the drop zone the jump master, having ensured that the correct heading, speed and altitude are attained, and that the drop zone sea conditions are acceptable, will give the command to go. Each swimmer in turn will reach out and grasp the bar, allowing his body to hang below. Mask and fins are looped over each arm and, facing forwards, each diver will swing his body so that it inclines slightly forward, at which time he will let go of the bar and grasp his fins and mask as he drops down into the water. As soon as he hits the water and comes back to the surface, he puts on his fins and joins the remainder of the team, to swim on to the beach.

For the pick up, the ladder is lowered down to a position about a foot above the surface of the water, and the aircraft flies slowly

Above Fast, well-armed tactical helicopters provide support to special forces.

Below Helicopters are used to deliver and recover combat swimmers. Two SEALs climb a ladder during a recovery operation.

down the line of swimmers, allowing each to grab hold of the ladder and climb up into the helicopter's cabin. The amount of equipment that can be carried by this method or on the fast water drop and pick up is very limited, and therefore the operational duration of the swimmers is severely restricted unless stores are cached or an RV has been established prior to infiltration.

When helicopters are used, the swimmers will be delivered to and picked up from the shore or suitable landing zone close to the operational area. The men can be deployed as swimmers or as fully-equipped divers. Amongst the aircraft available are the CH135 Hueys and CH147 Chinooks. The former carries up to six swimmer/divers, whilst the Chinook carries up to twenty, with the ability to make a low level rapid deployment through the rear door. Both aircraft use rope ladders for recovery, but the Chinook can lower is rear ramp into the water, thus allowing the swimmers to crawl aboard. Even fully equipped divers can be recovered in this manner.

Helicopter support comes from the two US Naval Reserve Helicopter Attack Squadrons, who fly HH 1K gunships. The helicopters are fitted with M21 weapons, in the form of 2 GAU – 2B/A Gatling Guns, two rocket launchers carrying seven 70 mm (2.75-in) folding-fin aerial rockets (FFARs) and two door-

Above The SBS and SAS would have available the Lynx helicopter which is fast and can be equipped with weapons for a combined strike role.

Below Soviet Spetsnaz use the Helix twin-rotor helicopter, as well as larger gun ships.

mounted M60 machine-guns. The crews train in the use of night-vision goggles, which enhance their ability to extract teams at night, providing them with fire support if necessary.

Swimmer delivery vehicles

The use of underwater vehicles to deliver swimmers is not new, for they were used very successfully in the Second World War. Use of such vehicles in the 1980s is shrouded in great secrecy and from those on the inside come blank answers ranging from 'we don't use them' to 'no comment'. What is evident and beyond doubt is the fact that Britain does have such craft, as do many other nations. The Soviet Union in the past few years has used at least two types of manned mini sub, one free-swimming, the other tracked for movement over the sea bed. The United States of America has dedicated Swimmer Delivery Vehicles (SDV) teams, and used them in the Vietnam war.

There are two main types of underwater vehicle, the 'wet' SDV and the dry lock-out mini submarine. Both have the same aim, that is to deliver the swimmer to a target, and to carry a payload greater than would be possible by the swimmer on his own. The first category is the 'wet' vehicle which, by definition, means that the swimmer and controls are open to the surrounding water. The size of such craft varies from the two-man basic unit to the four- and six-man more complex unit.

Swimmers lie on, sit on or in, the vehicle while it moves through the water. The swimmers are dressed in their underwater swimsuits and breathe through the closed-circuit UBAs. The equipment fitted to the vehicle will vary, depending upon the task and recent technical developments, but it will carry the basic navigation and depth instruments, along with an acoustic transponder/receiver. Depth control is critical, since the swimmers will be using underwater breathing systems with strict limits on diving depths. This restricts the options open to an SDV trying to evade detection, or penetrate an anti-submarine net. The basic two-man vehicle is designed around a cigar-shaped tube which houses the batteries, propulsion unit and buoyancy tanks. The instruments and guidance controls are added on, allowing

Above A combat swimmer lies on a towed sledge for covert drop off or sweep searches.

Below A two-man swimmer delivery vehicle of the WWII chariot type.

Above Swimmer wearing closed circuit breathing apparatus using small vehicle to travel through the water.

Right A cigar-shaped SDV which is flown by one swimmer and can tow another. Note the instruments fitted at the bow.

Below right The SDV can be fitted with numerous items of equipment for intelligence gathering. Note lights and cameras.

the swimmer/pilot to lie on the vehicle to fly it, whilst the other swimmer is towed on the aft section. The main role of this class of vehicle is for attack against maritime targets, when the swimmers and a payload of mines can be ferried to and from the target.

The operational capability of this unit will be governed by the swimmers' UBA duration and the craft's battery power supply. Being small and lightweight, the vehicles can be carried by a parent submarine to a drop-off point, where the swimmers exit the submarine as described earlier, and with the aid of the casing divers, prepare the craft for operation. The craft can be conveyed inside a special garage, or attached to the hull of the submarine. Either way, the swimmers can depart the parent craft and set a course for the designated target. The parent submarine can drop a transponder beacon on to the sea bed and depart to another location. The swimmers may raise the vehicle to the surface and travel under cover of darkness towards the target. Once submerged they will navigate the final phase, raising only to check bearings. Once the mines have been attached to their target, the vehicle will be steered out to sea, to RV with its parent craft.

The use of these vehicles means that the hard work of swimming against tide and current is eliminated, resulting in swimmer teams being more flexible in the target area. The vehicle will use its transceiver to locate the beacon position, from which it will receive a course bearing to follow, to locate another beacon fitted to the submarine. The need for the submarine to move and set up its beacon on a separate frequency is in case of capture of one of the teams, which could allow the enemy to get a fix on the waiting boat. Voice communication between swimmers on the outside and the crew on the inside will be established, and the vehicles secured before the swimmers re-enter the submarine.

The larger and more complex 'wet' SDVs can carry four or six men, with a considerable payload of weapons or stores. The power and duration of these larger vehicles enhances the operational and flexibility requirements of the swimmer teams. They can carry additional underwater breathing equipment and have the capability of energizing swimmers' electrically-heated undersuits. Again, these larger vehicles are carried to the target area by a parent submarine, which allows the teams to transfer whilst submerged, thus not risking compromising the operation.

The range of operations that can be undertaken by these vehicles is considerable. They can carry swimmers into a harbour or dock area and act as a base, allowing the swimmers to clamp limpets on any number of targets, returning to the vehicle for more mines when needed, and finally exfiltrate them from the area. Carrying teams underwater, they can slip into enemy-held territory, unseen and unheard. The combat swimmers can be dropped off or the vehicle can be set down on the seabed and made safe, whereupon the men will swim ashore to land under cover of darkness, and move inland to undertake a task. When completed, they swim out to the vehicle and make for an RV at sea.

The SBS would find the vehicle of great use when undertaking beach survey and reconnaissance, for apart from exposure on the tide line, they could remain unobserved. The flexibility of the vehicles would enable a number of

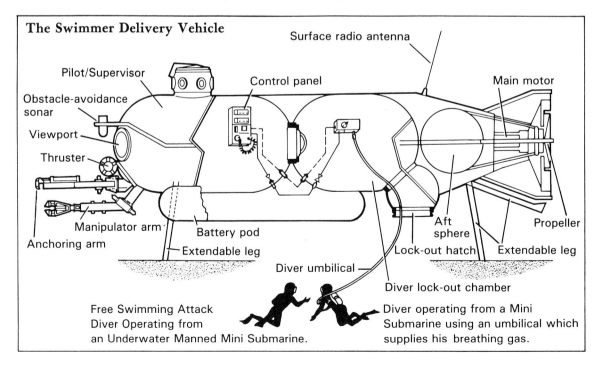

The Swimmer Delivery Vehicle

Surface radio antenna

Pilot/Supervisor

Control panel

Main motor

Obstacle-avoidance sonar

Viewport

Thruster

Manipulator arm

Anchoring arm

Battery pod

Extendable leg

Aft sphere

Propeller

Lock-out hatch

Extendable leg

Diver umbilical

Diver lock-out chamber

Free Swimming Attack Diver Operating from an Underwater Manned Mini Submarine.

Diver operating from a Mini Submarine using an umbilical which supplies his breathing gas.

beaches to be surveyed in the time it would normally take to do one. The advantages of these craft in an amphibious landing can be found in the laying of beacons on the sea-bed which the landing craft or assault ships could follow, providing them with a clear passage, especially in darkness, and allowing rapid deployment ashore of the assault forces. Swimmer raiding and recce groups can be resupplied by the vehicles; meeting on a quiet stretch of beach, supply packages would be collected by the OP party, who would then disappear back inland whilst the SDV swimmers rejoined their parent submarine.

Perhaps the most intriguing of the underwater vehicles are the 'dry' mini submarines. An insight into this world can be seen through the development of craft for the commercial market in the deep oil and gas fields throughout the world. Here financial resources for development have been available which, in the military context, only war conditions would normally have permitted. This is not to say, however, that a pure military machine has not been developed.

The 'X' craft, mini submarines of the Second World War, were towed to the target area by the parent submarine, then whilst on the surface the crews transferred and departed on their raid. Today, the submarine will not want to venture onto the surface unless it has to, and with the manned mini submarine of today, this is not necessary.

The mini sub is divided into three basic areas. The first is the control area, from which the pilot flies the craft. It is fitted with all manner of electronic devices, from compasses to obstacle-avoidance sonar and depth-recording equipment, to the mass of controls informing him of the vehicle's status regarding power, oxygen supply and purity and accurate positioning.

The second section is a chamber which can be sealed off from the first, allowing the swimmers to pressurize it to equal the outside water pressure, so allowing them to exit the craft. When they have completed their task they can re-enter the chamber, seal the outside door, and return the chamber's inside pressure to equal that at the surface. The advantages of this type of SDV are found in the depth the vehicle can travel to avoid harbour defences, whilst not exposing the crew or swimmers to the external pressures, and also keeping them dry and warm. The vehicle would raise itself to the lock-out depth at the target, and would wait on the sea-bed for the swimmers to return, each in turn tracking the other with underwater beacons.

The third section of the craft contains the propulsion unit, which is powered by batteries, these being stored in two large pods on either side of the vehicle. Oxygen in high pressure bottles is also carried on the outside of the craft, and carbon dioxide scrubbers keep the internal atmosphere clean and safe. Transporting the vehicle is by sitting it on the deck of a submarine, the mini sub's mating hatch being set against the parent sub's hatch, then secured for travel at sea. The addition of a vehicle on the parent craft would affect the streamlining and reduce its speed, but once on location, the crew and swimmer team could transfer from the submarine's escape chamber up into the mini sub, which would then be free to disengage, and depart on its mission. Deep-water penetration and the setting of anti-submarine sonar buoys are examples of the mini subs' capabilities, and alongside the 'wet' SDVs, their use will increase in the coming years as a means of infiltrating highly-trained special forces troops.

As far as is known, no swimmer delivery vehicles were used during the operations in the Falklands' conflict. A number of reasons can be put forward for this, and one could well be the speed of mobilization of the Special Boat Squadron, whose members were the first elements to depart south, and who undertook wet parachute drops to rendezvous with submarines. The next reason could have been weather conditions, for the majority of SDVs leave the swimmers open to the sea and operate in shallow water and at a constant depth. The

A dry mini submarine being manoeuvred to fit on to a parent submarine. The swimmers are kept in the dry and can lock out into the water to undertake on operation.

sea state was unpredictable and could have jeopardized both craft and swimmers. Kelp was another problem that could have influenced the decision, as very prolific beds surround the islands. From a study of these points, and from experience gained from the US landing on Grenada of specialist amphibious units, a number of important factors have been raised on present swimmer delivery vehicles and their future development.

The factors that have become relevant are that they must be small and lightweight, capable of relatively high sustained cruise speeds and undertaking long-range operations. The ability to operate away from a parent craft or support unit for extended periods of time combines with the considerations needed for the deployment and recovery of the vehicles, and the parent craft should not be subjected to abnormal danger. Reliability and ease of operations, along with payload, are extremely important factors to be considered in the design criteria.

We can therefore see the Swimmer Delivery Vehicle requirements as being an operational range of at least 200 nautical miles, with a cruise speed of ten knots. The operational duration of the vehicle at cruise speed should be twenty hours, plus 24 hours at the target, with 350 man hours of life support, which does not include the emergency reserve. There should be emergency power in hand for halfway-point return. A major factor is the depth capability, which for diver lock-out needs to be from the surface to 60 m (200 ft). The transit depth during operations would be 150 m (500 ft) and the depth capability for the vehicle, unmanned and in transit on a mother submarine, would be 390 m (1,300 ft). An operating crew would number two men, and within the payload capability of 900 kg (2,000 lb), eight divers/swimmers could be carried, if it is assumed that a diver with his equipment weighs 113 kg (250 lbs). Delivery of the vehicle to the drop off zone could be by surface ship, mother submarine or heavy lift helicopter. The vehicle would need a mission turn-round time of not more than 24 hours.

Perry Offshore Inc, a US company, have extensive experience in the research and development of sub-sea vehicles, both military and commercial. They have undertaken trials on tank models using a design based on proven large submarine configurations, and as a result they have produced an overall package which may go some way to providing the military with the vehicle that they require to fulfil their operational needs. The task is to utilize off-the-shelf components wherever possible, to ensure proven reliability, but this is not always possible when seeking to produce a new concept. Research has pin-pointed two configurations for possible development: the first is the Deep-

Discharge Lead-Acid Battery propulsion power unit, the second is the Closed-Cycle Energy Source Propulsion Power Unit.

The advanced concept Deep-Discharge Lead-Acid Battery powered vehicle has an overall length of 13 m (43 ft) and a beam of 1.8 m (6 ft). Its displacement is 27 tons, and the power source produces a cruise speed of ten knots. The advantages of this concept are low cost, least technical risk, low acoustic signature, reduced design complications, and the fact that it utilizes established technology. On the disadvantage side, it has a reduced operational capability, a large hull, and although it can carry the same payload at the same speed, it has an operational range of only 100 nautical miles.

The Closed-Cycle Energy Source powered vehicle has an overall length of 10.6 m (35 ft) and a beam of 1.8 m (6 ft). Its displacement is seventeen tons, and it can cruise at ten knots, with an operational range of 300 nautical miles. The principal advantages are the very high energy/density unit. It is the smallest and lightest of the proposed designs, and can operate within the desired range and depth criteria, carrying the required payload. On the other hand, the disadvantages are that although the engine is established technology, it is not in

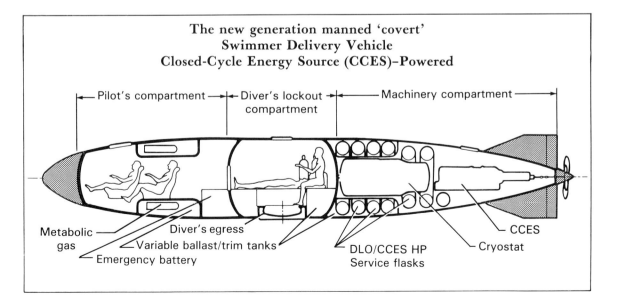

The new generation manned 'covert' Swimmer Delivery Vehicle Closed-Cycle Energy Source (CCES)–Powered

Subskimmer moves at high speed.

production, and there are technical risks; the acoustic signature is also greater.

A general description of the CCES unit is that it is a propane-fueled, rotary, internal combustion engine using liquid oxygen as an oxidizer and helium as a dilutent. The CCES concept also uses a mechanical scrubber for carbon dioxide removal, in lieu of the bulky chemical absorbant beds. The basic problems at present are that a suitable production unit has yet to be assembled, and the use of the mechanical scrubbing unit for this application has not been proven. The internal combustion engine is noisier than the battery-powered systems and will need to be damped. Perry are confident that they can overcome these problems and so present the military with a viable SDV that can deliver covert divers/swimmers to their operational target.

Previous insights into the use of Swimmer Delivery Vehicles have shown that the parent craft, most probably a submarine, would need to gain very close access to the target area, thus submitting it to a high degree of risk. With this problem in mind a unique system has evolved from the workshops of Submarine Products in the form of the British-designed and built Subskimmer.

Based on a proven military rigid hull inflatable, and powered by an outboard engine, it can be converted, in about a minute, to a self-contained, submerged swimmer delivery vehicle, with two electric thrusters producing two and a half knots underwater, and with an operational duration of up to six hours from its own battery power supply.

The main hull is rigid, with inflatable tubes fitted as in a more conventional raider. Power is provided by an outboard motor of some 85 hp, which is encased in a pressurized waterproof housing, and it has an exhaust system which is closed prior to submerging. The requirement for a large engine on such a small craft is because of the all-up weight carried, in the form of batteries, air cylinders, pump equipment and the underwater propulsion unit.

Transformation from surface craft to SDV is via a powerful suction-pump housed in the centre of the craft. When the team requires to submerge, they seal the outboard's exhaust and activate the pump, which sucks the air out of the boat's side tubes, collapsing them, and allowing the boat to become awash. The final de-ballasting is done through the pump housing. In the bow, the pilot sits behind the swivelling motor tube, and once awash, he can start the two electric propulsion units, one at either side, which enable him to fly the craft in either direction or up and down, by simple hands-on control. In front of him, in the cross tube, are housed the instrumentation in the form of log, speedometer, timer, compass, echo sounder, amp and voltmeters and the power switches. The 1 kw power thruster units pull the craft through the water at a speed determined by visibility, combat conditions and possible obstructions. Power for the thrusters comes from two separate 5 kw hour banks of batteries.

Subskimmer is able to carry four men with limited equipment for a range of some 100 miles at a speed of 25 knots, combined with a final underwater operational capability of a range of six miles at two and a half knots. If a heavy stores load is carried the crew is reduced to two, but the load could be in the form of additional fuel pods, which will extend the range considerably. All members of the crew would be dressed for underwater swimming and, when on covert operations, would use closed-circuit underwater breathing sets.

The possibilities of this craft are immense, and for countries without a submarine delivery system, it opens new doors. Subskimmer has a length of 5 m (16.4 ft) and an unladen weight of 800 kg (1,764 lb) so it is well suited to being carried by a fast patrol boat or fishing boat for surface delivery, and once launched can speed away towards it target. Palletized in the same manner as the inflatable raiding craft, it can be parachuted into the operational area and, as already discussed, be joined in the water by parachute swimmers. In enhanced helicopter operations it would be ideal as a delivery system for the craft and the crew. With Subskimmer being a submarine as well as a surface craft, it can be carried wet by a submarine in an 'add on' garage. At the drop-off area, the swimmers lock out of the submarine to join the craft submerged. Once aboard, they can fly clear of the submarine and surface sufficiently to carry out an observation; if all is clear, they can inflate the tubes, start the outboard engine and move on the surface at an operational speed towards the target area.

From the same workshops as Subskimmer comes a highly versatile and compatible closed-circuit oxygen system, called Oxymagnum, which the manufacturers claim has an operational duration of up to six hours. This combination of craft and diving system would allow swimmers to proceed to the target on the surface at a speed dictated by combat circumstances, and when necessary transform the vehicle into an SDV, allowing the final phase to be underwater. The vehicle's electrics can be shut down to allow the swimmers to depart to defined targets where use of a craft is impracticable.

Because of Subskimmer's flexibility, it can be used in all environments, from Northern Norway to the Middle East and Africa, and in quantity for large amphibious operations or in pairs for more covert reconnaissance missions. Their use in ship and harbour attacks would enhance the swimmers' survivability and success ratio.

Withdrawal from the combat area could be undertaken submerged, then awash and finally on the surface, at slow speed initially, then at increased speed once clear of the enemy's observation posts. The rendezvous with the parent craft, whether submarine, surface vessel or helicopter, would find the crew less fatigued that with some more conventional methods of transportation. It is prudent to remember the operational care needed for a submerged RV with a submarine, in so far as battery power is concerned, for the boats may have to be written off, if unable to be recovered because their batteries are drained. That would probably be an extremely small price to pay against the value of a successful mission, however.

SEAL teams utilize a wide range of vehicles and equipment in their operations, which may not be readily available to the SBS and SAS who have similar operational roles. The need for flexibility in underwater operations has produced a number of developments, especially for working in extreme climatic conditions, for long endurance swims to a target area. The first problem has been partially solved by the development of specialist underwater equipment and by advances in scientific knowledge of man's survival problems in cold water. For extended combat swimmer operations, the continuing development of Swimmer Delivery Vehicles means that these craft have a greater range and carrying capability than before, and vary in type of modifications, depending upon the task for which they are to be used.

All SDVs have the same basic characteristics of ballast, propulsion, an electric motor adapted for use underwater, a hull and equipment to control depth, direction of travel and the basic overall ability to carry swimmers underwater on a covert mission. The advantages of using the SDV are numerous, and begin with the very basic one of being able to move a number of men further and faster than they could achieve by free swimming. Of course they are able to transport a far greater load of stores. These advantages have to be weighed against the need to train skilled SDV operators to fly the craft, and the need to adapt the parent submarines required to deliver the vehicles into the operational zone.

The majority of US SDVs are 'wet', which means the swimmers either sit in or on the vehicle, and use underwater breathing apparatus, as they are open to the surrounding water. In the covert attack role the swimmers will wear closed-circuit underwater breathing sets, and if using oxygen great care will be needed to keep the craft within the operating depth limits. It is possible for the swimmers whilst in the open sea to use compressed air on open circuit, changing over to closed circuit when calm water could mean detection.

All of the listed SDVs are of US design and development and have a wide range of mission capabilities. They can be used for reconnaissance, intelligence gathering, insertion and extraction of special forces teams, and to undertake swimmer attacks against the enemy. The vehicles can save on swimmer endurance, and carry a large store payload of combat weapons, including limpet mines, or equipment for on-shore missions.

The SDV MK VII-Mod 2 is a four-man, wet, submersible vehicle, constructed of glass-fibre and non-ferrous materials to minimize acoustic and magnetic signatures. The instruments and electrical components are housed in sealed watertight containers, and are designed for ease of use and maintenance.

SDV MK VII-Mod 6 is an upgraded version of its predecessor and still carries four men, but is improved for greater operational capability and to carry additional weapons and navigation equipment, including obstacle avoidance detectors, which give more flexibility in rendezvous and docking. As with the Mod 2, glassfibre and non-ferrous materials are used.

The EX VIII SDV is again a wet submarine, designed to carry six swimmers and their equipment. As with the other vehicles the swimmers are in a sea environment, and use an onboard breathing system or their own closed-circuit sets. The vehicle is driven by an electric motor, powered by rechargeable batteries, the latter controlling the vehicle's endurance. The craft carries a computerized Doppler navigation system, an obstacle-avoidance sonar and a system for rendezvousing with the parent craft.

EX IX is a two-man combat swimmer SDV which can operate either below surface or on the surface as a conventional boat. The vehicle carries the same advanced systems as its larger brothers.

More than one SDV can be carried by a submarine, so a major underwater mission can be undertaken. A vessel such as the USS *Grayback*, a diesel-electric submarine converted for special operations, has a hangar for the smaller delivery vehicles, and can carry some 65 specialist troops, with the SDVs being utilized as a 'taxi service'.

Chapter 12
Equipment

Augustus Siebe, who had founded the firm of Siebe Gorman and Co, died in April 1872. His sons took over and continued the work already begun. The firm became involved with H. A. Fleuss, a British inventor, in 1878 and from that time they co-operated to produce the first practicable self-contained breathing apparatus, based upon the regenerative principle, using compressed oxygen and a carbon dioxide absorbant. Although the unit could be used underwater, interest came from those involved in mining and areas using toxic gasses.

R. H. Davis joined the firm in 1882 and worked under Henry Siebe and W. A. Gorman, where he remained to become Managing Director and to eventually take full control of the firm in 1924. Development work had continued, and prior to the First World War, Davis and Fleuss had developed two systems, the Proto and the Salvus, which the British and Americans used in mines. The first underwater interest came in the possible use of the equipment to escape from a stricken submarine, and to this end development proceeded. The Davis Submerged Escape Apparatus was the product accepted.

Siebe Gorman moved quickly to the forefront of underwater technology, and when the company became the headquarters for the Admiralty Experimental Diving Unit, they pro-

Salvus underwater breathing apparatus.

duced the Amphibian Mk I. This apparatus comprised a steel cylinder which was charged with pure oxygen, a carbon dioxide absorbant chamber, a mouthpiece, flexible hose, breathing bag, goggles, noseclip and a lead weight for ballast at the back. It was soon superseded by a modified version which incorporated new developments, such as twin cylinders on the back. These systems resulted in the production of the Universal Breathing Apparatus, which was based upon the Amphibian but able to utilize oxygen or an oxygen/nitrogen mixture.

New inventions in underwater craft required different equipment for the operator. The charioteers did not need to be free swimmers, but did need to keep warm during their long periods in the water. In 1942 Siebe Gorman addressed the problems with Captain G. M. Sladen, DSO, DSC, RN, who was in charge of the human torpedo-chariot project.

Experiments with the users who were under training found the best results were achieved when the charioteers wore silk underwear next to the skin. Kapok padded jerkins and trousers were next, with woollens put over the top. Finally, the waterproof suit. Hands created a big problem, as all developments with gloves were unsatisfactory. Many of the divers and swimmers used 'Peddo' grease.

The original charioteer's waterproof suit was of lightweight rubberized cotton cloth, with a headpiece. The faceplate was an ordinary Service respirator, bonded into the headpiece. The big problem with the suit was that when the diver was dressed he could not open the face plate, and this hampered his operational use.

The Mk II suit was developed with a hinged metal face plate, so that the wearer could have it open on the surface and could close it easily when going under water. It was also made wide enough to allow the use of night binoculars. To extend the operational range of the chariot a modified set of breathing apparatus was developed, which enabled the operators' oxygen bottles to be carried as part of the torpedo, the diver having a small personal system which would allow him to make good an attack when he left the craft.

The 'X' craft required a different suit from that of the charioteers, for the diver would be in the water for a relatively short period, and he also needed a flexible suit, as he had to dress and undress in a confined area, and use the cramped escape chamber to exit and enter the craft. Two suits were developed from modifications to the Sladen equipment, one for the divers, and a lightweight one for the watchkeeper when the craft was on the surface.

The 'P' parties, formed to remove mines from harbours, docks and rivers, had other problems. They were dealing with many magnetic mines, so every part of their equipment had to be non-magnetic. This entailed the use of aluminium alloy cylinders, and valves, buckles and other fittings to be made from non-ferrous metal, whilst knives were produced from non-magnetic steel. The mine recovery suit was two-piece and had a self-contained helmet system, which was able to utilize oxygen/nitrogen mixtures for working in deeper water.

Even the canoeists of the Special Boat Section required a different suit. They did not have to have breathing apparatus for reconnaissance of enemy beaches, so a waterproof suit with an inbuilt inflatable life jacket in the upper part was produced. It included various pockets for compass, watch, maps, charts, scribbling pad, pencil, emergency rations, revolver and ammunition and a knife. A waist belt carried the measuring line and stake.

The frogmen's suits were developed in conjunction with the Dunlop Rubber Company, and the process was similar to that used today. Rubber was spread on to stockinet, to produce the body of the suit, which incorporated latex rubber cuffs and plimsoll rubber feet. The rubber neck yoke was highly stretchable to allow the swimmer to enter. The neck seal was made by clamping a latex hood to the neck yoke. Hoods and face masks were produced by a latex dipping process. Experiments continued all of the time with undersuits, goggles, swim shoes and camouflaged swim suits. Italian suits were made from thin black rubber sheet, finishing at the neck. They were light and easy to wear, but afforded little protection against the cold, and were very easily damaged.

Today, equipment carried by individuals will be a mixture of personal choice, and like many regular and reserve troops, they will purchase some of the variety of civilian survival and foul weather items to add to their issue list. For operations, swimmers/divers will wear full combat uniform, suitable for the terrain and climate of operation. In this uniform they will carry automatic pistols in shoulder holsters, plus a number of personal survival items stowed in pockets. The underwater dry swimsuit is worn over the top, and has not differed greatly from that worn during the Second World War.

The materials used in producing today's suits are a natural rubber, spread on to a two-way stretch knitted nylon fabric. They have zipped rear entry, which means a second swimmer is needed to close or open them. The flexible rubber seals at the neck and wrists exclude water, thus, in theory, keeping the wearer dry. For operations in warm climates, and for short duration operations, a thin lightweight front entry dry suit is available, allowing each swimmer to dress or undress himself without assistance. The nature of this suit, being made of thin rubber, makes it susceptible to damage. Whichever suit is worn, the swimmer cannot wear his onshore boots, so these are stuffed into the pit of the back prior to zipping up. Ashore, the swimmer can remove the suit, put on his boots, and be ready to take up an onshore role.

The other underwater swimsuits available to the swimmers today are the wet suit and the Uni suit. The wet suit is manufactured from a closed-cell expanded foam, neoprene, which is a synthetic rubber-like material, full of minute cells which are separate and sealed to water ingress. This suit is close fitting to the swimmer's body, and allows water to enter between the material and the body. This film of water is heated by body heat and so produces an effective form of insulation. Because of the cellular structure of the material, the suit is buoyant, and if torn is easily repaired, allowing cold water to af-

The modern dry suit seals at neck and wrists.

fect the damaged area only. The big disadvantages are that the swimmer's body is 'wet', and in extremely cold weather conditions this could subject the swimmer to hypothermia after leaving the water; it will reduce the swimmer's in-water time as well.

Nor is the wet suit particularly good for parachuting, as it tends to grip the webbing, and be pulled, making it uncomfortable for the wearer. Because of its ease in use it is used for wet parachute training, however, and boat work where limited endurance and good weather are the order of the day.

The 'casing divers' who support the submerged submarine lock out operations use another type of suit, the Uni suit. This is comprised of foamed neoprene, similar to that of the wet suit, but is sealed at the wrists and neck to keep the wearer dry. Its thermal insulation qualities go a long way to help keeping the diver warm.

The operational attack swimmer will have depth restrictions imposed, depending upon his breathing mixture. Pure oxygen is the most common breathing gas for the attack role, but it has a depth restriction of 10 m (33 ft), and for most underwater attack operations this is adequate. The swimmer requiring to operate at deeper depths, as could be the case when exiting a submerged submarine or using a swimmer delivery vehicle, can use a mixture of nitrogen and oxygen (nitrox). The mixture used depends upon the deepest operational depth, but comes in standard mixes: surface to 10 m pure oxygen; surface to 25 m (82 ft) 60% O, 40% N; surface to 42 m (138 ft) 40% O, 60% N; and surface to 55 m (180 ft) 36% O, 67% N.

The SBS have recently changed their underwater breathing apparatus after exhaustive trials, for a new system that meets their exacting requirements for a set which is as small as possible and totally front-mounted, as well as being rugged in construction, as it will be subjected to the rigours of parachuting, canoeing,

A close-fitting foam neoprene wet suit.

and being humped over land, stuffed in a Bergen, or buried on some quiet beach. Endurance is a prime factor, and the new system from Dräger meets all of these requirements, apart from the fact that, being enclosed in a plastic shell for protection, it is bulky when stowed in a Bergen. However, it does provide the swimmer with some three hours' underwater operating time, and also falls in line with standardization policy within NATO's combat swimmer groups.

The SBS swimmers use a half-mask with their system, which they find more practical as it can be removed easily, whilst not affecting the breathing. The mask has a low profile and allows a swimmer to use a camera when on a beach recce. It also reduces the drag factor when work-

ing outside a submerged submarine, which may be moving slowly ahead to maintain headway. Another valuable point is that on a clandestine underwater attack, the swimmers will be in pairs, and if one should experience problems with his breathing set, they can buddy breathe; that is, share one breathing set, thus not compromising the mission or giving away the fact that an attack is under way. This system also has an inbuilt buoyancy, which is useful on operations where both sea water and fresh water can be encountered as the different specific gravity of each affects the buoyancy of the swimmers.

The Royal Navy Diving Branch uses the Diving Set Self Contained Clearance Diving (DSSCCD), or as they refer to the original title, the Clearance Diver Breathing Apparatus (CDBA) or Clearance Set Mark 3. It is the system used by the Special Air Service's boat troop swimmers, but unlike the SBS's separate mask, the CDBA has a full face

Dutch Marine Combat Swimmers using Dräger LAR V breathing apparatus line up target with compass for underwater swim.

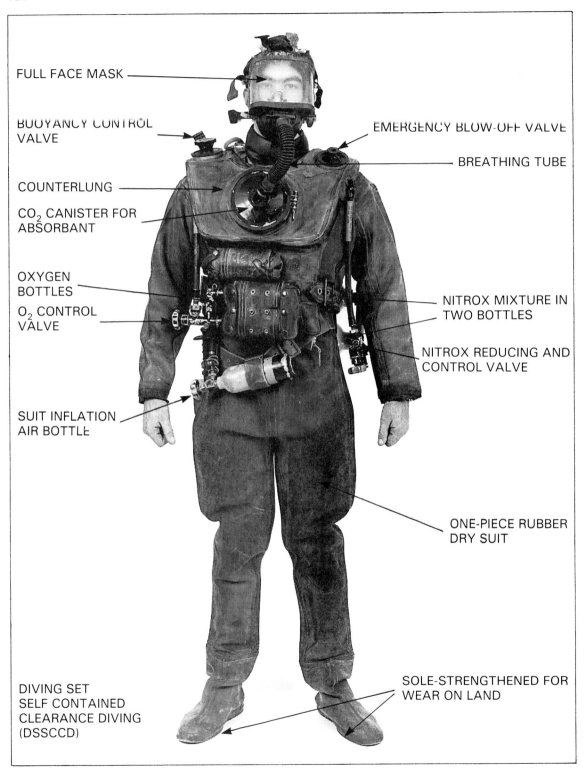

FULL FACE MASK

BUOYANCY CONTROL VALVE

EMERGENCY BLOW-OFF VALVE

BREATHING TUBE

COUNTERLUNG

CO_2 CANISTER FOR ABSORBANT

OXYGEN BOTTLES

O_2 CONTROL VALVE

NITROX MIXTURE IN TWO BOTTLES

NITROX REDUCING AND CONTROL VALVE

SUIT INFLATION AIR BOTTLE

ONE-PIECE RUBBER DRY SUIT

DIVING SET
SELF CONTAINED
CLEARANCE DIVING
(DSSCCD)

SOLE-STRENGTHENED FOR WEAR ON LAND

mask, with a mouthpiece incorporated.

The duration of these sets is governed by the carbon dioxide absorbant, which is activated when the swimmer charges his set and begins to breathe. From that moment, he has ninety operational minutes. To extend that time, the absorbant would have to be replaced. Spare absorbant can be carried in sealed containers, but the swimmer has to get into the dry and remove the apparatus, to empty and refill the canister. This sits on his chest, with the counter lung either side. The Navy retains the full face mask in the belief that if the swimmer should 'black out', which is very possible with the closed-circuit system, the mask will remain in place, as will the mouthpiece, and so keep the swimmer supplied with a breathing mixture. With the half-mask system, the mouthpiece could be lost, resulting in the swimmer drowning. Thus each unit uses the system most appropriate for its operation.

In the early days of the Commando commitment to Norway many problems were experienced, from contending with the severe cold, to lack of specialist equipment, and limited experience in snow survival. The SBS suffered, and in fact still do in some cases today when the extreme cold freezes things quickly. They had cases of carbon dioxide poisoning with swimmers who were well within the endurance of the closed-circuit underwater breathing sets; it took some time to find out that in extremely cold conditions the carbon dioxide absorbant does not work so efficiently, and as a result expired gas is not fully scrubbed.

The Standard Diving equipment went out of general use in the RN some twenty years ago, and was replaced by the Surface Demand Diving Equipment (SDDE). This consists of an open-circuit self-contained breathing apparatus, but instead of the diver drawing air from two

Left A Royal Naval attack diver in closed circuit oxygen breathing apparatus DSSCCD.

Right The standard diving equipment has long been replaced in the Royal Navy.

Royal Naval diver using surface demand diving equipment
(SDDE) with communications, and the Aquarius compressed
air set as a reserve.

high-pressure cylinders, the supply comes from
the surface, by way of a compressor or a bank of
large high-pressure cylinders. The cylinders carried by the diver will only be used if the main
supply ceases. Being open circuit, the expired air
containing carbon dioxide passes through a
valve and into the surrounding water. The basic
set for this equipment is the Aquarius, with the
surface supply added. It is very suitable where
duration and shallow depths are involved.

The Aquarius air diving set replaced the
Sabre air diving set during a phasing-out period
in 1976–8, and consists of two compressed-air
tanks, joined by a manifold which has a reducing
valve on it. This reduces the high pressure air in
the tanks to low pressure for the diver to breathe,
and the reduction is balanced to provide the correct pressure of air to the corresponding depth.
This is an automatic process and does not require adjustment by the diver. The tanks are in-
verted and the diver can reach the open/close

valves by reaching back with his hand. Since
divers often work in poor visibility or at night,
they may not be able to use a contents gauge to
see the pressure of air in the tanks, so they use a
decanting system. One of the tanks is opened
and breathed from. When the pressure is reduced and it becomes difficult to breathe the other
valve is opened, which will allow half the contents of the remaining full tank to flow into the
empty one. The valve on what was the full tank
is then closed. Continuing to breathe from the
original tank, until it becomes difficult to
breathe, divers then open the valve on the other
tank, and know that on the second decant it is
time to leave the job underwater and come to the
surface.

The underwater closed-circuit breathing
set comprises of a gas cylinder, filled with the appropriate mixture, which supplies a flexible
breathing bag, the counter lung. The counter
lung is subjected to the same pressures as the
diver's lungs, so he can breathe easily, regardless of depth, but should the gas build up in
the counter lung, it has a relief valve fitted which
is held closed by a spring and the external water

pressure. The valve will lift if the counter lung pressure becomes slightly greater than the pressure holding it closed. Set into the bag is a canister which holds the carbon dioxide absorbant, and from the canister comes the concertina rubber breathing hose, which can go direct to the swimmer's mouth (SBS mode) or into the full-face mask (Royal Navy/SAS).

With this system the breathing gas, which can be either pure oxygen or an oxygen/nitrogen mixture, is contained in the cylinders at high pressure. When the swimmer opens the cylinder outlet valve, gas at high pressure passes to a reducing valve, where it is converted to low pressure and passes on to fill the counter lung. The swimmer breathes in, pulling gas from the counter lung, through the carbon dioxide absorbant, up the rubber hose to the mouthpiece and on into the swimmer's lungs. Upon expiring the breath, the gas returns down the hose, through the carbon dioxide absorbant, where the carbon dioxide is scrubbed from the gas, which returns to the counter lung where it mixes with fresh gas. The procedure is continued, with the gas being scrubbed twice. Breathing through this method of a single hose and absorbant canister is known as 'pendulum breathing'. The disadvantage is that a 'dead space' exists between the mouthpiece and the canister, and the small amount of gas trapped in this section of hose is breathed back into the lungs, having been expired and not passed through the absorbant. To minimize the possibility of carbon dioxide poisoning, the swimmer must breathe deeply and normally. In some breathing sets, a twin set of hoses is used, where gas, having passed through the absorbant, is drawn by inhalation up one hose into the lungs and then out through the other hose into the absorbant canister. Prior to the swimmer entering the water, the counter lung is charged with gas, and breathed down, to be recharged again. This is to ensure the system is working correctly, and to remove the nitrogen that may be in the system from being on the surface and open to the atmosphere. The swimmer will descend to just below the surface, where he will check the breathing, and his team members

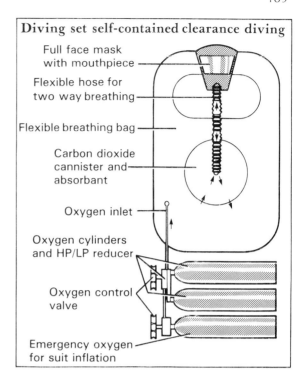

Diving set self-contained clearance diving

Full face mask with mouthpiece

Flexible hose for two way breathing

Flexible breathing bag

Carbon dioxide cannister and absorbant

Oxygen inlet

Oxygen cylinders and HP/LP reducer

Oxygen control valve

Emergency oxygen for suit inflation

can check that the system does not give off any bubbles, indicating a leak in the set. Once the swimmers are checked, they set their swimboards' compass bearing.

The Emerson closed-circuit oxygen rebreathing apparatus, referred to simply as the 'Emerson', was used until recently by both the former UDT and SEAL teams, but they now use the Dräger LAR V system, in line with other NATO special forces underwater units. The Emerson has a 0.36 m³ (12.7 cu ft) oxygen cylinder which can be charged to 2,000 psi. The carbon dioxide absorbant canister contains 2.7 kg (6 lbs) of absorbant, providing an operational duration of 120 minutes. The unit weighs about 16 kg (35 lbs) out of water and is neutrally buoyant underwater. Similar to the system used by the SBS, it utilizes a half-mask and separate mouthpiece. The layout of the unit provides oxygen into one counter lung breathing bag, from which the gas flows up a flexible hose to the mouthpiece and into the swimmer's lungs. Breathing out, the valve system only allows the expired gas to flow down the exit hose, to pass

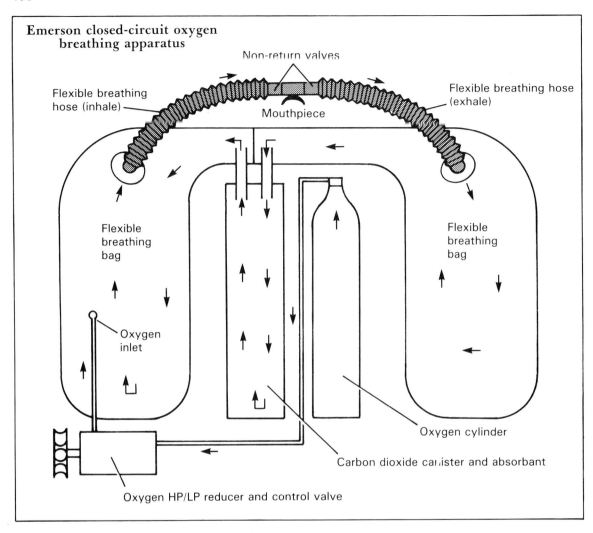

Emerson closed-circuit oxygen breathing apparatus

Non-return valves

Flexible breathing hose (inhale)

Mouthpiece

Flexible breathing hose (exhale)

Flexible breathing bag

Flexible breathing bag

Oxygen inlet

Oxygen cylinder

Carbon dioxide canister and absorbant

Oxygen HP/LP reducer and control valve

through the carbon dioxide absorbant and into the other breathing bag. The two bags are connected and the gas is circulated, with the oxygen fed in to replace that breathed and absorbed. As with all closed-circuit systems, no bubble discharge is given off and the usual depth limitations apply.

A no-bubble system may be needed for quiet and still water areas, but in the sea, along beaches and on submarine operations, the discharge of gas is not so critical. A modified Dräger system has therefore been introduced, fitted with an exhaust valve that diffuses the gas to a stream of fine bubbles. Using a mixture of

oxygen and nitrogen, swimmers can operate to a depth of 21 m (70 ft), and the system extends the carbon dioxide absorbant's life to 180 minutes.

SBS and SAS swimmers, wearing their combat suits and armed with a personal survival weapon, have at their disposal a vast range of support weapons, depending upon the task. The Ingram MAC II is probably the smallest automatic weapon available, weighing 1.6 kg (3.5 lb) and able to fire twenty rounds per second of 9 mm ammunition. It has a high fire rate, but when fitted with a suppressor to silence the noise and flash it has an accurate range of only some 50 m (55 yd). The heavy Heckler and

Koch MP5 also fires 9 mm ammunition, but has a range of 200 metres. It is the latter that has found a dedicated place in the armouries of both SBS and SAS. For greater firepower, the M16 Armalite rifle is available. Firing 5.56 mm ammunition, its firepower can be further enhanced by the fitting of a grenade launcher. For large assaults against a defended target the teams can be augmented by heavier weapons such as the GPMG and anti-aircraft and anti-tank weapons. The individual weapon still favoured in open expanses of terrain is the SLR (Self-Loading Rifle), as it has a greater hitting power at longer ranges. The new SA 80 Individual Weapon (IW) and the SA 80 Light Support Weapon (LSW) are now in service with the

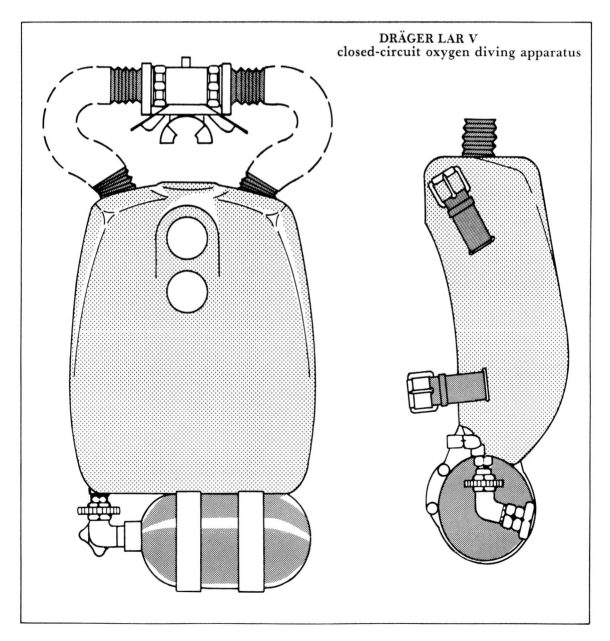

DRÄGER LAR V
closed-circuit oxygen diving apparatus

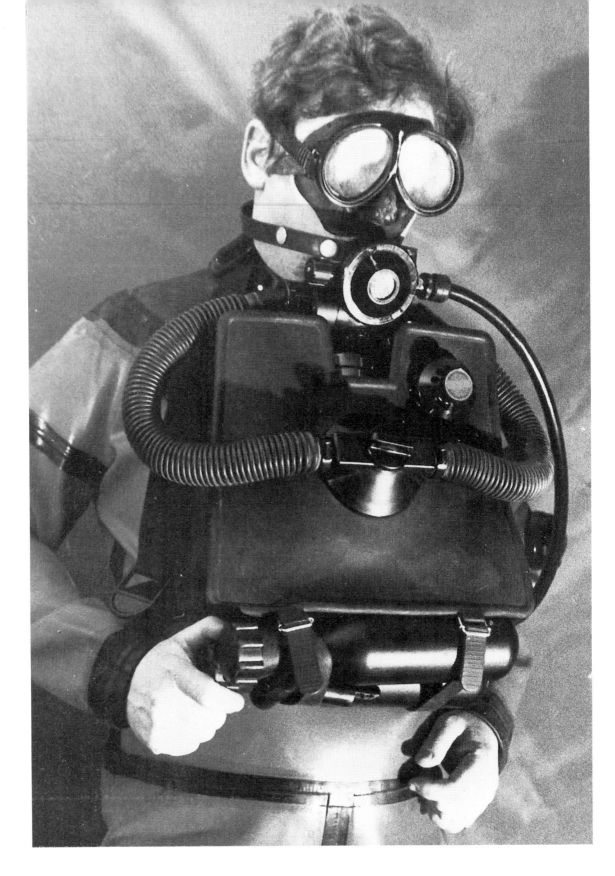

Above SBS swimmers carry a wide range of weapons, and the 9mm Browning is a personal weapon for each man.

Top The SA-80 individual weapon in service with the British armed forces is an ideal special forces weapon.

Left The modern Oxymax closed circuit oxygen breathing set produced for combat swimmers.

British armed forces, and will certainly find their way into the swimmers' armoury.

The clothing and equipment of the Soviet special forces is adequate but basic. Their backgrounds are more frugal and they are generally more accustomed to hardship than the average NATO soldier, but not more so than NATO's special forces. Until quite recently Soviet soldiers wore foot cloths, called Porlyankai, which were wrapped around the feet under boots, although these have now been replaced by socks.

Rations are limited in issue, and are not in special packs, as Western troops receive them, but are basic food stuffs, so any supplementary food must be foraged for, along with fuel for fires on which to cook the food. It must be expected that, by nature of the Spetsnaz role, rations and cooking abilities must improve, if they have not to date. The Soviet Special Forces troops travel light, carrying weapons, ammunition and their personal items of clothing. General field survival equipment such as sleeping bags and waterproof shelter items appear to be almost non-existent. The following quotation describes some of the special forces' equipment.

The loaf of white bread and two hefty tins of stewed meat and some fish have to be tucked away further so that they do not press against one's back. Poncho, cam-suit jacket, spare footcloths, mess tin, spoon, a small net, hooks, a fishing line, matches, a wire-saw, packets of explosives, cartridges, a torch, bandages, cotton wool, and tubes of disinfecting tablets have to be placed in separate sections of the kitbag. The flask of water, the folding spade, the small axe are hitched on to the belt. On the right hip the pistol. We also have AKMs with silencers; a machine-gun, two RPG-7Ds, two radio sets and a set of batteries, a set of flares, magnetic and other mines, special instruments and devices for their destruction.

Chapter 13
Bombs and mines

As we have seen, the naval diver still has a role as an attack swimmer, but the cessation of training in escape and evasion, and lack of parachuting and submarine lock-out skills reduces their operational effectiveness. One reason for this may be the rapidly-developing role of naval divers in the expanding mine counter-measures field. New and updated vessels carrying full clearance diving teams are joining the fleet, taking over from the 'Ton' Class of minehunter.

Included among the equipment carried on a mine-hunter is a one-man decompression chamber, needed because of these vessels' far-reaching operational areas. The first of the new mine hunters was a 'Wilton' Class, constructed of glass fibre in 1974. Today divers can look forward to the new single-role minehunter; designed for extended operations, they will be constructed of glass reinforced plastic. They are

Britain's modern mine-hunting ships can find themselves operating throughout the world, and provide new challenges for the diving teams aboard them.

tasked with keeping the sea lanes, docks and harbours free to allied shipping, so in the Royal Navy's NATO mine warfare counter-measures sphere of operation, the naval divers will be tasked with clearing paths through minefields. With this role in mind, the clearance diving set has been modified to ensure that the over-pressurization pop-off valve is set to allow a very fine discharge of minute bubbles, to allow the diver to deal with finely-adjusted acoustic mines. The equipment is completely non-magnetic, using rubber and plastic where possible, and phosphor bronze for metal parts.

Should a mine-hunting vessel detect a mine in a hazardous area, the divers would move to its location using the Gemini inflatable boat, whereupon a diver would enter the water and descend to the spot indicated, where he would search for the object or objects and mark them off so that they could be dealt with. The diver could subsequently place a charge on the mine and after leaving the water, detonate it. Alternatively, a remote-controlled vehicle could fly to the object, drop an explosive charge, and then move clear to allow the charge to be detonated. Because of the large number of mines that would be laid, sweeping tactics would be used before individual mines were sought and disposed of,

Right A Royal Navy clearance diving team looks on as a mine is blown up after a diver has placed an explosive charge on it.

Below Dutch divers enter water from a mine hunter as part of NATO's mine warfare commitment.

but many mines are placed in locations where conventional sweeps would not find them.

Hunting for mines is not restricted to British or NATO waters, but extends to friendly countries who need to utilize the expertise of the Royal Navy's mine counter-measures units. Recently mine-hunters were dispatched to the Suez Canal area where mines had been laid in shipping lanes, and had to be cleared. This gave enormous operational experience to the crews of the hunters and to the clearance divers.

A major role both for clearance divers and for ships' divers is in the defence of ships, and the removal of any devices that the enemy may place on them. The first and most favoured type of mine is the magnetic limpet, which a diver

Below and right Two Royal Naval underwater search devices designed to help locate objects in dirty water conditions. Either a visual signal or sound systems provide the diver with information.

places against the steel hull, then departs, the timing mechanism allowing a suitable time lapse before detonating the charge. When a diver finds such a device, his first task is to try to identify it, then to leave the water and advise the Diving Officer (DO) of its location and description. The Diving Officer then has to make a decision, for it is possible that there will be more than one device to deal with. In the case of the magnetic limpet he has several choices, the first being to use the anti-explosive unit, which works on a similar principle to the tracked unit used by the Army on land. It comprises a hollow tube which is filled with water, and into one end a cartridge is fitted. This is fitted with an electric circuit and is fired in safety from the surface. The diver takes the unit down and fits it to the hull with a magnetic clamp so that the tube points at the centre of the mine. The cartridge is fired, pushing water at high pressure into the thin skin of the mine, through a pin-prick sized hole. Once inside, the water disperses and blows the

explosive out, at such a speed that it beats the detonation of the mine, rendering it safe. Most mines will have an anti-handling device fitted, so pulling the mine off is not practical, although it may be possible to slide a thin sheet of steel down between the hull and the mine. As a last resort it may be possible to attach a line to the mine and use a boat on the surface to pull if off, hoping that when it detonates it will not do a lot of damage. Other mines can be clamped to a ship's bilge keel, and are primed and detonated by the movement of the ship through the water turning a propeller, in much the same way that an aerial bomb is primed.

The Soviet limpet mine is plastic-cased and weighs 3 kg (6.6 lb). Its charge of TNT with a high aluminium content combines with an RDX booster and can probably blow a 3 m (10 ft) hole in heavy steel plate. The time fuse is of a delay type, and can be set to anything between five minutes and over a month.

Any ships of the Royal Navy plying the seven seas can call upon the clearance divers if required. The Fleet Team based in the UK has its team members ready to go to any part of the world, and their equipment is air portable. Such support could be to assist ships, or to aid a friendly country which may have a bomb or mine problem.

Wherever a device is found, either in mud, black murky water, or clear water around a ship's hull, the diver still has to deal with an object which, if it detonates, will kill, even if he is not very close to the explosion. We have seen earlier that the 0.45 kg (1 lb) scare charge used by the Navy in anti-diver operations can kill, and the diver may well find himself dealing with a 450 kg (1,000 lb) bomb that is not in a very stable state.

It is an interesting point of fact that SBS and SAS swimmers are normally a reserved group of people, partly due to the severe restrictions imposed upon them for security reasons, whereas the naval clearance diver is more ex-

trovert and often more than a little on the strange side, but in a different way. The attack diver/swimmer knows the tasks, is briefed, and will be trained in most eventualities, but the naval explosive ordnance disposal (EOD) diver may be tampering with a large quantity of high explosive. Moreover, the people who delivered it in the first place will not want him to 'play' with it and may well have set traps. There are different types of courage, and one type of swimmer/diver may shake his head at the other, perhaps not envying him his job.

One story exists of a naval diver at an ordnance range, who was bored with things, being with members of the Army with whom he did not have a great deal in common. So he ambled about, and seeing finned objects sticking out of the ground began rather idly to kick them. This continued for a while, and when he turned to look at the soldiers, they had disappeared. Our matelot followed in the direction that they would have taken to find them in the bottom of a hollow with their heads down. Once they regained their composure it was explained that the range was used for live firing and that the fins he had been kicking were attached to live mortar bombs which had not exploded. The response from the still bored matelot was to bury his hands deeper into his pockets, shrug his shoulders and mutter words to the effect that he had never seen a mortar bomb. The soldiers watched in amazement as the sailor moved off looking for one to examine.

Dealing with unstable explosives is part of the diver's lot, for most things left in water will corrode, exposing the contents to the elements,

Explosive devices are often found on the beaches, and involve the Royal Navy Bomb Disposal team.

and it is usually in this unstable state that they will have to be dealt with. The locations of such devices are many, from holiday beaches to laying alongside oil pipelines in the North Sea, for even today mines and bombs from the Second World War appear and have to be dealt with.

The wailing tones of the police car's siren will alert those in the area, and curiosity will be roused as the car speeds past, blue light flashing and headlights on full beam. The curiosity will be directed not so much at the police car but at the dark blue long-wheelbased Land Rover following close behind. Its unusual appearance will be enhanced by the large inflatable boat lashed to the top, and the words, stark white on the dark bodywork, ROYAL NAVY - BOMB DISPOSAL. As police car and Land Rover come to a halt, no crowds will gather round, as the local police force will have cleared the area of sightseers, for as far as they are concerned the object washed up on their beach is suspect, and if a bomb or mine, could cause untold damage if detonated.

This situation can and does occur on every beach in the United Kingdom, some more so than others. It is the task of the Royal Navy's diving branch to respond to an emergency call, which may result in a long drive to the suspect item. The diving teams are based in naval bases at Portsmouth, Plymouth, Portland, Rosyth and Clyde. They are equipped to answer the call by road travel, and with them in their vehicles goes the underwater diving equipment. The divers of these teams change round with other teams, and may find themselves on a mine-hunter or deep-diving vessel.

Through the Tri-Service organization of Explosive Ordnance Disposal (EOD), the Navy along with the Army and Royal Air Force have teams ready to react. The Navy usually deal with a mine washed up on a beach or brought ashore in a fisherman's net, but if a Royal Engineer team with divers was in the area, then they would tackle the problem, as it all boils down to a spread of limited manpower over a large area.

The officer in charge, 'the Boss', in the Royal Navy, will along with the Chief (Chief Petty Officer) site the object and if possible define what it is. Today the majority of explosive devices washed up on beaches are relics of the Second World War, and most are in good condition and extremely lethal. Whilst the Boss, Chief and head of the local police force discuss the possible solutions, the remainder of the team will begin preparing some of the equipment that could be needed. One option open to them is to detonate the object on the beach, but this could shatter all the window panes in the local shops and houses. They could disarm the fuse mechanism, then remove the bomb or mine out to sea and detonate it in a safe location; or if the item or items are small, they could carry them to the Land Rover and take them to a range, where they could be disposed of safely.

The large German wartime mines are almost spherical in shape, with horns sticking out which, if stuck, cause detonation. Bombs and mines of Second World War vintage are well known, and the EOD man has a lot of background and training to allow him to deal fairly safely with them, but it is the modern, unknown devices which cause concern. On the surface, television cameras can survey an object long before the 'man' has to approach, but under the water, in mostly black, murky, muddy conditions, the diver will have to grope around, defining the object by touch, for when he returns to the surface he will have to give a detailed account of what is below. In the case of the clearance and disposal carried out in the Suez recently, the mines were Soviet acoustic models, so retrieval was paramount in order that the West could assess them, even though they were not of a recent vintage.

Searching docks and ships is of obvious importance in the 1980s, and the demand is increasing. The most recent high-security operation was on the P & O cruise-liner *Royal Princess* at Southampton, where teams of divers searched the hull and surrounding dock area for explosive devices. Arrival at this type of job is low profile, without the flashing blue lights and wailing sirens which herald arrival at a seaside holiday resort to deal with a wartime mine.

Experiments with the use of hovercraft for mine counter-measures operations on beaches and in shallow water have continued for a number of years. Whilst the West has not developed the craft in any particular form or quantities, it is interesting to note that the Soviet Union has expanded its numbers of hovercraft. Capable of moving on both water and land, the hovercraft has a small pressure footprint, and can move over anti-tank and anti-vehicle mines in relative safety. It can also provide support for swimmers at sea, as well as traversing the mud

and soft sand found on some beaches. That support may simply be in the form of a base and a platform for carrying away unwanted finds, but hovercraft can also provide fire support, as they can be armed, although they are somewhat limited in size of firepower. Future development and use of hovercraft appears uncertain, however, as financial restraints will prohibit full exploration; even the Royal Navy's hovercraft unit has now been disbanded, and its craft disposed of to civilian companies.

A notable piece of ordnance disposal was undertaken in 1970 off the Island of Jersey by the Plymouth Command Clearance Diving Team. They were called to investigate the wreck of a German freighter, sunk by the RAF in the last war. It was the cargo that was of concern, for the vessel carried a variety of ordnance which over the years had deteriorated. More than fifty 450 kg (1,000 lb) bombs made up her cargo, and they were found to be rusty and almost unrecognizable. The corrosive effect of the sea had rendered the bombs, primers and detonators very unstable. For the Navy's clearance divers it was just another job, and the fact that the sea conditions were poor, with both a heavy swell and virtually no visibility, was quite normal. One added problem was the leakage of iron pyrites from the primers; this is a volatile substance and therefore extremely dangerous, since the slightest knock or even temperature change can cause detonation.

The disposal operation was to be divided into two parts, with the first lasting five weeks. The initial survey determined the condition of both vessel and bombs, and from this the plan of action was drawn. Care had to be taken, for the lives of the divers and of the civilians some one and a half miles away were at risk. Some of the divers would no doubt have commented that their own lives were probably a long way down the list.

The weather was not good, and the heavy swell created by Atlantic gales hampered operations. The depth in which they worked ranged between 12 m (40 ft) at low tide to 21 m (70 ft) at high tide. They used both wet and dry suits,

Mines come in all shapes and sizes, and require divers to locate them, identify the type, and place charges so that they can be destroyed.

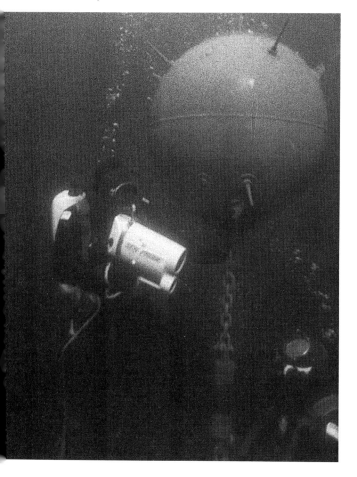

and the Clearance Divers Breathing Apparatus, with an oxygen and nitrogen breathing gas. They dived at the turn of tides, for one hour at low water and forty minutes at high water. They had to work quickly and efficiently, for time was not on their side. The efforts during this phase resulted in the raising of 23 bombs, which were lifted individually, taken aboard the diving vessel, and further out to sea, where they could be detonated safely.

Phase two was not going to be so easy, for amid the tangled wreckage of the ship's hold were about fifteen bombs far too dangerous to be moved. They would have to be detonated in such a manner as to cause as little shock wave as possible. The charges had to be placed by divers entering the hold amidst the twisted jagged steel. The work done, the area was cleared and the charges detonated. For those on land it was an anti-climax, since the ground shock was minimal and there was no air blast to create a loud bang. For the Clearance Divers it was a successful completion to a difficult job, earning them a commendation.

For the islanders, especially the inhabitants of St Helier no more than a mile and a half away, there was satisfaction at the removal of thousands of pounds of TNT, which could have put at risk the mass of tourists who frequent the area.

Overleaf The Plymouth command clearance diving team dealing with a cargo of dangerous explosives aboard a sunken vessel off Jersey.

Below Experiments using hovercraft for mine counter measures operations were undertaken by the Royal Navy.

Chapter 14
Terrorism

Offshore oil and gas rigs are not the only potential targets of terrorist attacks; Britain's first 'water' anti-terrorist operation involved a ship. The *Queen Elizabeth II* was in the Atlantic, having left New York bound for Southampton. A phone call announced that bombs had been planted on board and that a ransom should be paid before the location of the explosives would be given. The ship had a full complement of passengers and crew.

Rapid decisions had to be made, and the first act was to deploy Nimrod aircraft to remain over the ship, both to monitor the ship's progress and control a rescue operation if the threat were carried out. The next decision was quite simple: if there were bombs on board then the priority was to get bomb disposal men on board and render them safe, or at least contain the explosion to a known area, for the crew's search had revealed nothing out of the ordinary. A Hercules C130 transport aircraft of the Royal Air Force departed from the UK carrying four EOD experts. Two men were from the Royal Marines Special Boat Squadron, one was from the Special Air Service Regiment and the fourth was from the Royal Ordnance Corps; the latter was not only making his first parachute jump, but into the Atlantic Ocean to boot!

The men jumped in pairs, the SBS men first, the SAS and Ordnance man second. Watched by crew and passengers on the liner as she wallowed in the Atlantic swell, the four men were picked up by the ship's boats, along with their equipment, and taken aboard the liner. A detailed search of the ship found no bombs, and the phone call was put down as a hoax, or by somebody hoping that a payoff would be made against a threat. One thing was learned from the action, and that was that from the beginning, Britain would not succumb to terrorism.

On land the terrorist situation is less complicated to handle, as seen within Europe, and especially dramatically in London at the Iranian Embassy, where sophisticated electronic equipment in the form of fibre optic cameras and ultra-sensitive listening aids can provide valuable information. Then if and when action occurs, the full facilities of the emergency services are immediately to hand, especially if any hostages are injured. Manpower can be moved to observe the target and control the situation by use of night vision equipment, and snipers can be positioned to take action if required.

At sea, the problem is totally different, and to some extent to the advantage of the terrorist. In 1985 Arab terrorists struck another blow at the maritime industry, when the Italian cruise ship, *Achille Lauro*, was seized. The crew and passengers were held hostage for two days, and subjected to a campaign of terror, culminating in the murder of a disabled American passenger, Leon Klinghoffer. A US Navy SEAL team was placed on stand-by and began preparations to carry out an underwater rescue mission, which could have involved the use of a shaped explosive charge to cut their way through the ship's hull, or fast boat and helicopter insertion if the ship did not stop. In the event, the terrorists negotiated for the ship's release, negating the need for combat swimmers and underwater vehicles.

On 18 May 1986 a tip-off was received by the police that an Arab terrorist group had planned to drive a car, fitted with explosives, on to a cross-channel ferry and detonate it in mid-channel. A thorough search was instigated, and proved negative, which was just as well, for the effects of a ferry disaster were visibly apparent with the loss of the *Herald of Free Enterprise*.

Tourists aboard the 600 ton Greek ferry *City of Poros* were caught in a terrorist attack close to the Island of Agenia on 11 July 1988. Grenades were thrown amidst the passengers, causing panic and leaving 11 dead and almost 100 wounded. It was another ill-conceived action, which could easily have had far more serious consequences.

To counter such possible action on one cruise to the Mediterranean, again involving the *Queen Elizabeth II*, SBS men first scoured the hull for any devices, then put away their diving equipment, donned civilian clothes and mingled with the passengers, their personal armament hidden, but ready to use. Each time the vessel docked, the swimmers would keep watch and ensure that nothing was planted on the ship that could jeopardize the safety of those on board. It would be wrong to visualize a high life for the men, attending parties every night, for the terrorist will strike at the enemy's weakest point, and that would be when the revelry was at its peak. It would be then that the SBS men would need to move into action, either on board the ship, or by having to endure long periods of time under the water, searching for mines or other explosive devices.

Whilst passenger ships have been the main targets for terrorists so far, the transportation of 'risk' cargo is a growing concern. Today a wide range of volatile and dangerous cargoes are transported. None of these vessels is immune

from terrorist attack. Consider the scenario of nuclear fuel in the form of plutonium nitrate solution, loaded in special 250-1 containers from Dounreay in Scotland, moved by road to a nearby port, and loaded on to a ship for the two-day sea journey to Workington. The containers are designed to withstand any possible accident, but not necessarily a shaped explosive charge. If such a vessel were then sailed into a high-density population area – Liverpool, perhaps – the threat of explosive destruction would present authorities with unacceptable consequences.

It was during the early to mid-1960s that a new and very vulnerable target for the terrorists began to appear, in the form of offshore gas platforms in the southern sector of the North Sea, and later oil platforms in the northern sector of the North Sea. These structures come under the jurisdiction of the police, namely the constabularies of Great Yarmouth in Norfolk and Aberdeen in Scotland, as these steel and concrete islands are considered part of the UK.

The number of structures has increased over the years, and in the northern sector they have become larger, with more people living on board, resulting, in security terms, in a bigger problem. The control of manpower going offshore is limited by the fact that the numbers of men involved is large, and the oil companies look at the commercial aspect of the operation first, so that terrorism is regarded like any other emergency, to be dealt with as and when it happens.

With a work-force that includes a lot of sub-contract labour from a considerable number of nations, who have neither work permits nor authority controlling them, the problem is very real. On one rig, a new diver joined the civilian diving crew. He was Irish and showed a great deal of keenness as he enquired about the make-up of a rig, and was in turn shown the various construction drawings, from which he made sketches. He was also able to procure other useful information about platforms, their workings, gas and oil output and manpower numbers, all of which was carefully noted.

This man had worked in Scapa Flow under-

Above and right On board the platform, the 'terrorists' must be found quickly. Note: automatic rifles and infra-red sights. Once found the terrorists are disarmed and taken captive.

taking underwater demolition, so was very familiar with explosives and the storage of such material. He had a collection of manuals on the subject of explosive demolition, booby traps and others which would be expected on the book-shelves of a professional terrorist. This diver openly stated that he had served in Long Kesh prison in Northern Ireland, was a supporter of the IRA and totally anti-British. The facts were presented to his employer in Aberdeen, whose only action was to shrug the matter off and place the man on another rig. This contracting com-pany employed many foreign personnel and this was just another case where supplying man-power came before any form of security.

The oil rigs and platforms in the North Sea are under the jurisdiction of the Civil Police Authorities, and in a security emergency, com-mandos from Comacchio Group Royal Marines, based at Arbroath in Scotland would be made available to the authorities. This group is made up of specialist commandos, and it would be fair to assume that the unit is familiar with the plat-forms in the North Sea and with amphibious swimmer operations. A specialist force will need to be equipped with sophisticated and specializ-ed weapons, as well as a wide range of transport, from Rigid Raiders to helicopters. Private com-panies can only pursue the line of 'prevention being better than cure', and where possible, for-mulate security advice for those prepared to ac-cept it.

In an article in January 1987's edition of *The Oilman*, a theory was promoted that the cap-size of the flotel *Alexander Kiellands*, in 1979, was due to sabotage. The allegation, put forward by a Norwegian engineer, claims that explosives were used to damage one of the rig's legs, caus-ing it to break away. At the enquiry into the

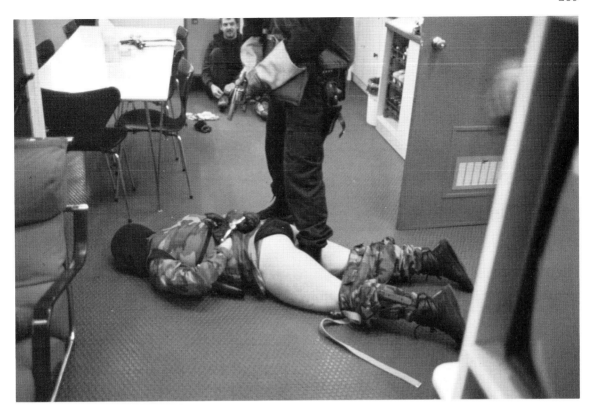

disaster, survivors reported that they heard a sound like an explosion before the rig began to list. One hundred and twenty-eight lives were lost.

Probably a major factor in the fact that no terrorist action has yet been made using divers stems from the fact that, whereas a terrorist can be taught how to use weapons and fieldcraft, it is a much harder skill to learn the art of clandestine attack diving with closed-circuit breathing apparatus. Many countries base their military diving on the British system, as over the years Britain has trained many foreign personnel in diving. This activity has slowed down over the last few years, as it is somewhat difficult to determine your friend of today, enemy of tomorrow. In any event, though, it would be prudent to assume that terrorists will become trained in the use of this specialist equipment.

The manufacture of underwater bombs or mines is easy for the terrorist organization which has experience of doing this on the surface. It really means waterproofing the bundle, and that can be done with a plastic bag. There is no need to go to a great depth and a raid can be carried out by competent underwater swimmers in about 3 m (10 ft) of water.

The Navy accepted this possibility and as a result HMS *Maidstone* was sent to Northern Ireland as the Navy's main base. Her men and small craft had an anti-terrorist function, especially in preventing gun running. The off-duty and support staff lived aboard the ship, which was in fact a submarine depot ship and had ample accommodation and facilities. It was also used, during its stay, as a prison ship, retaining terrorists caught on the mainland.

Part of the team on board were men of the Royal Navy's clearance diving branch, who were tasked with the ship's underwater defence. An anti-escape and attack boom was placed around the ship, and the divers checked this boom at regular intervals, as well as the hull of the ship, for penetration by terrorists. The SBS on the other hand were given the job of breaching the security screen and leaving behind mementoes of their visit. This was of benefit to both parties, and no doubt each was determined to outdo the other. When the *Maidstone* left and the prisoners moved to conventional prisons, the Navy's role in counter-terrorist activities diminished as far as Northern Ireland was concerned. However, both the RN and Royal Engineers divers have been tasked with regular searches of sewers, rivers and lakes for the weapons of war used by the terrorists.

Weapons and explosives can be infiltrated by boat, having the package fixed underneath the hull, or a boat could drop a sealed package into the sea, with a small marker displaying its location. Amid a fisherman's inshore fishing grounds it would be difficult to locate. In both cases divers could be used to recover such packages, and it is a field of operations that can be expected to expand. Today the RE divers have the task of sewer inspection, where they look for weapons, explosives and the movement of terrorists themselves. This aspect of operation is very dangerous, as the terrorists can place remote controlled devices, and detonate them when troops are down in a very confined space. If the divers find anything, it is an extremely difficult environment in which to deal with a device.

If the terrorists do develop skills in underwater attack and start such operations, it will certainly cause the authorities more than a few problems. Ships of importance, such as the Royal Yacht *Britannia*, are prime targets, and reservoirs, bridges, power stations, dams and, of course, docks, both civilian and military, are all vital and vulnerable targets.

Chapter 15
Mammals and robots

Mammals at war

Some 90 kg (200 lb) of sleek streamlined mammal moves effortlessly through the water, cruising at six knots, its inbuilt sonar seeking out that which should not be there. Amid the warships and cargo carriers berthed in the naval dockyard, the patrol below the water's surface continues, silent and efficient.

The enemy mini sub had left its parent craft and moved up into the dock area, evading the outer defences. Then it bottomed out and the enemy underwater swimmers put on their equipment, and prepared their mines. When they were ready they entered the chamber that allowed them to equalize the pressure to the water outside. In the murky darkness of water the swimmers, in pairs, adjust to the environment and check compass directions. They then begin the swim to selected targets, the leader of each pair breaking the surface only long enough to get a fix and seek out any hazards. They then continue, their fins pushing the water behind them as they move, encumbered by the weight of the limpet mines they carry.

Above, the guards of the United States Navy base will have seen and heard nothing of the attackers, but under the water, in the gloom of muddy water and night-time darkness, the guardians have sought out the intruders. No recognition signal emits from the attackers, and as all friendly swimmers carry these, they are automatically deemed to be 'enemy'. Moving effortlessly through the water at a conservative speed, the creature of infinite beauty and of an intelligence level next to man, uses its sonar to make the final adjustment and powers itself up to a speed of some thirty knots. The distance is short, but far enough, as the entire weight of the dolphin rams the enemy swimmer. Communication between the dolphins enable them to each single out a target. Within moments, swimmers are destroyed, their mines fall uselessly to the bottom of the dock, unarmed. The dolphins, having disposed of the enemy swimmers, break the surface, alerting the guards. Trained not only to destroy the targets, they then retrieve the bodies to the surface, where the guards in boats are able to recover them.

Alerted, the defence organizer dispatches another of the dedicated underwater search group. This time the dolphin uses its sonar to search the harbour bottom, to seek out the delivery vehicle, then when found, it moves forward to meet it. The mammal is encumbered with a harness, onto which is attached a limpet mine. Through a communication link between dolphin and controller, the command is given and the dolphin moves in alongside the mini sub, which is making an exit from the target area. The dolphin rolls effortlessly over as it passes the craft, and the powerful magnets grip

to the steel hull, simultaneously releasing the mine from the harness. The dolphin rises to the surface to indicate that the explosive device has been delivered. Both man and mammals return to the safety of the dockyard and their pens.

The mini sub rejoins its parent craft and both move out to sea, knowing their teams of assault swimmers have been lost, but not how. The vessels now have to evade the enemy who is searching for them. The detonation at sea of an explosive device is recorded and a search by warships in the vicinity finds no survivors, only debris, found to have come from an enemy submarine.

*   *   *

The submarine, specially converted, moves towards the enemy coastline and the harbour approach. Numerous warships and cargo carriers are preparing to leave, as they are part of an amphibious assault group, full of men and equipment. The submarine moves to its final destination and the Captain hands over the final stage to the special group of men who are part of the mammal attack unit. The conversion of the submarine allows four dolphins to be carried in safety and comfort to the drop-off zone, where they are fitted with special harnesses to which powerful anti-ship mines are attached. Equalized to the external pressures, combat swimmers move with the dolphins as they leave the safety of the submarine. The years of careful training and planning come to fruition as the graceful beasts depart the swimmers and move towards the distant dock. The harness slows the mammals down, as their sonar seeks out the harbour entrance and the distant ships. Diving deep they pass any anti-diver devices and move in amidst the steel hulls of the enemy ships. Their movement through the water has left no trace, and alongside a ship, a mine is clamped on, armed with the movement through water as the dolphin

swims to the target. It detaches from the harness allowing the next mine to be deposited. The four dolphins each carried two mines and now as they departed the dock area, eight ships are primed for destruction. The excited clicking of the dolphins is heard by the submarine and the boat's underwater swimmers lock-out to meet them. Aboard the submarine, mammal and man are at one again, and, their harnesses removed, the dolphins receive a reward. The submarine departs the area, diving deep and running fast to avoid detection and be well clear of the area when the charges detonate, sending eight ships to the bottom of the sea, their cargoes of specialist assault troops and equipment lost to the next battle.

These two scenarios are, as far as is known, fictional, but there have undoubtedly been growing development and experiments between man and highly intelligent dolphins and small whales. In Forrest G. Woods' book *Marine Mammals and Man – The Navy's Porpoises and Sea Lions*, he makes some interesting points, and it appears that the first successful experiment with a dolphin was in the mid-1960s. It is also said that the US Navy's SEALs set up security defences around ports in Vietnam, and the patrolling of the underwater defences was undertaken by dolphins, which accounted for a number of enemy frogmen.

In 1965, two teams participated in the United States Navy's Deep Submergence Systems Experiments, living in the underwater habitat Sealab II. The second team participated in a more unusual experiment, with the assistance of a bottle-nosed dolphin called Tuffy.

The teams remained inside Sealab at a depth of 60 m (200 ft), and the experiments involved the men leaving the habitat wearing self-contained breathing apparatus to make excursions to collect samples and carry out experiments. The divers had two problems, the first being the conditions on the bottom, which were very muddy. It was highly likely that one of the divers was going to get lost. A lot of time was also expended with the divers returning to the habitat to collect tools and equipment, and they

SEALAB II was the underwater home of the first experiment with a bottle-nosed dolphin called 'Tuffy'.

were unable to return to the surface as they were 'saturated' and required extended decompression.

Training had been progressing for some time with dolphins, and those who conducted the experiments grasped the opportunity to put their protégé through its paces. The Navy set some tasks which the trainers decided could be accomplished, and Tuffy arrived with the chief of the dolphins experiment, two trainers and a veterinarian.

Tuffy had been fed a diet of cut pieces of fish, which was useful during the experiment, as the lights of Sealab attracted masses of fish, which the dolphin did not equate as food. The first task was to see if Tuffy could find a lost driver and assist him to return to the safety of Sealab. It was decided that the divers swimming through the mud should wear little electric buzzers, and the dolphin swimming on the surface would listen for these. When one sounded, it would dive down to locate the lost diver and guide him back to Sealab. Tuffy passed all of the tests he was given, and when not employed in demonstrations and training exercises, lived in a floating sea pen, which he left or entered upon his trainer's command. The rescue of a lost diver proved to be a highly viable proposition, even in darkness.

The next phase of the experiments was to determine the ability of the dolphin to act as a go-between from diver to surface crew and vice versa. This part of the exercise proved to be as successful as the first phase, and Tuffy was able to carry tools and other equipment between the surface and Sealab, and to the working divers.

From these beginnings it transpired that some people began to envisage squadrons of dolphins roaming the seas, seeking out enemy submarines then ramming them with high explosive charges. The one item of conjecture was whether the dolphin can differentiate between certain metals. If friendly submarines had a patch of special metal on their hulls, the porpoise could swim alongside, see the metal, identify it as being friendly and swim away. Those having no such patch would receive a mine, which

would blow the submarine to pieces. With a maximum cruising speed of some six knots, and hampered by a harness and heavy explosive device, it was envisaged that the dolphin would need to catch up and identify a submarine as friend or foe before destroying it. It would be a very imaginative Navy, however, that would entrust the safety of its submarines to a patch of special metal and impeccable judgement on the part of the attacking dolphin, and it would be an incredible dolphin that could swim fast enough to catch up with a modern nuclear-powered submarine, anyway.

The idea of suicide dolphins, carrying charges and ramming ships, generates a feeling of revulsion amongst most people, and from a military stand-point they would be an uncontrollable weapon system which could just as easily launch itself against a friendly vessel. Guarding harbours or attacking enemy shipping is pure speculation, and it is for the reader to review the situation and draw his own conclusions.

Underwater robotics

If the use of mammals is considered unacceptable in underwater warfare, then how will man fare as he expands the role of the underwater warrior in the future? For the combat swimmers aboard the delivery craft and for the defenders of harbours and 'water' targets, the war may eventually be fought with robots.

Squadrons of Spurs, which are patrolling underwater robots, would not be out of the question; indeed, with the rapid development of computers it is a reality and the developers of Spur have overcome many of the early technical problems. In a defence role, a number of Spurs can be transported to an area of operation by a surface ship, and launched in appropriate locations. The craft can then either remain in a fixed spot, their active or passive sonar seeking out enemy submarines or swimmer delivery vehicles, or they can undertake this role whilst patrolling. Control of the craft during this operation can be by either a shoreside centre or the mother ship. When a target is detected it has first to be identified, but once the fact that it is an enemy is confirmed, the robots can attack with torpedoes, or undertake a 'suicide' attack and ram an enemy boat, detonating onboard explosives. Swimmer delivery vehicles and swimmers can also be sought and eliminated, thus defending an important location whilst unseen by the enemy and safe from air attack, which would not be the case with a surface patrol boat.

In the attack role, the use of robotic vessels eliminates the need to expose highly-trained special forces swimmers to the dangers of acceptable, but the loss of special forces swimmers would not, and the swimmers are more suscepti-

ble to anti-swimmer defences, such as explosive charges and sonars.

Spurs can be carried to a target area by a 'mother' submarine, where the vehicles could be dispatched against a target. With a length of some 10–11 m (32–36 ft) and a height and width of 1.8 m (6 ft), they are hard to detect. They have a depth capability equal to any known submarine, and with modification, can attain a depth of some 6,000 m (19,700 ft) so they can approach a target clear of most defences. Endurance of up to two months allows them to be left in a harbour and during a tactical withdrawal phase, programmed to attack enemy shipping when it arrives. At a speed of twelve knots, Spurs have a round trip range of 1,000 nautical miles, or 2,000 nautical miles with drop tanks fitted. At the target the craft can achieve a speed of fifty knots, and attack the target with torpedoes or, if warranted, ram the enemy.

The SPUR can sit on the sea bed and await a target, listening with its passive sonar.

With its legs and equipment withdrawn, SPUR can move at high speed to carry out an attack.

Where the target is deemed large enough, it is possible to use Spurs on a dedicated one-way suicide mission; that would enhance the operational range to 2,000 nautical miles, or 4,000 nautical miles with drop tanks, and it could be fitted with a high explosive warhead. The price tag on such a craft would be in the order of £3 million, but this is very cost effective when compared with the cost of larger submarines and their crews which are required to remain at sea for long periods during hostilities.

Underwater robotics may be part of the distant future, and squadrons of Spurs may not be roving the seas for a few years yet, but technology exists today to develop an Advanced Concept Combat Remote Operated Vehicle (ACCROV), able to undertake covert beach reconnaissance, mine counter-measures, ship attack and defence.

A beach survey operation would begin with

the small operations submarine moving close to the shore-line, maintaining enough depth to remain hidden. Its cargo would not be a group of commandos or combat swimmers, but AC-CROVs, stored in transit garages on either side of the boat. The Captain would bottom his craft and, through the periscope, scan the beach for anything that could endanger the craft and its crew. It would be night-time, and the Captain would be aided by advanced night vision equipment. When he was satisfied that everything was secure, he would give clearance to the AC-CROVs' operators to begin their task.

Within the submarine, a control room with the latest state of the art of electronics will provide systems command function tests for the ACCROVs. Once these are completed, the garage doors are opened and the vehicles flown out. Although they free-swim through the water, they also have caterpillar tracks for crawling up on to the land. Capable of operating in currents of up to three knots, they are navigated by a low-light black and white TV camera, onboard sonar and navigation equipment. As they move towards the beach, their course is plotted, along with any obstructions or mines. The umbilicals pay out, providing control links with the pilots in the parent submarine. Depth readings are provided through the digital readout, and other information is recorded on video tape and still photographs. The cameras may be of an integrated system combining SIT low light, black and white television, a colour TV and a still camera, providing the three functions in one system. The vehicle is of a basic modular design with 'add on' equipment pods, depending upon the operation.

For the beach survey the ACCROV is fitted with the crawler pod, cameras, manipulator for taking sand samples, sonar and other advanced electronic equipment. Having completed its survey of the beach, the vehicle is backed into the sea and returns to the submarine, its valuable cargo of film and samples safe.

Prior to an amphibious landing a number of ACCROVs can be launched, fitted with a variety of 'pods', to crawl up the beach. Any obstructions can be primed with demolition charges, and coloured lights can be set up to guide landing craft. Other robots are fitted with machine-guns or rocket-propelled anti-mine systems, which when fired clear lanes up the beach allowing assault troops a mine-free passage.

Mine countermeasures warfare is a dangerous task, and ahead of amphibious landings even more so. The small submarine can be used in this role. Advance sonars can seek out minefields, and when in the area, ACCROVs can be launched, using onboard sonars and TV systems to seek, identify and plot mines. These can be primed with delayed action charges, allowing the submarine to navigate passages, then depart the area before the mines are detonated. Because these vehicles are used at a considerable distance from the parent craft, any premature explosion would destroy a machine, not men or the parent craft. In this role and others in a pure water environment, the vehicles would not be fitted with the 'track module'.

Could the attack swimmer be replaced by a machine? Using ACCROVs, enemy ships can be attacked in prime destructive locations. Sinking a ship in a dock requires great skill and daring on behalf of the combat swimmers, but a ship sunk in a harbour entrance may cause equal or more overall damage.

A harbour entrance is plotted with buoys which mark out the secure channel which shipping follows whilst in transit. A survey would look for a spot where the vessels slow down during navigation, and it is here that the submarine would head, equipped with anti-ship armed 'vehicles'. Moving as close as possible to the location, the submarine would find the safest position, at the maximum radius of the vehicle's umbilicals. The ACCROV moves from its base to a location alongside the channel where it sits on the bottom, using its passive sonar to seek out the enemy.

As a ship approaches, the pilot and operators aboard the submarine have to assess its value as a target. Once they decide to attack, the vehicle's active sonar plots the target, and it is raised, close to the surface where it stops at an optimum depth. It is equipped with four wire-guided short-range torpedoes, and the data fed from the 'plot' is transferred to the weapons guidance system. The vehicle is moved forward to the best position, and when the target is in line, a weapon is launched. The operators will also have to decide whether one, two or more weapons are used for the one target. The command wire pays out, with transmissions altering its controls until it strikes the target. After the attack, both vehicle and submarine shut down, and endure the enemy's search. Once this has passed the vehicle will be able to attack another target.

Defending a harbour from covert swimmer operations is a time-consuming and labour-intensive exercise, but each warship could carry one or two ACCROVs and special patrol boats could also carry them in defence modes. Advanced sonar will seek out SDVs and even swimmers. The robots would carry weapon pods to allow them to deal with intruders, and would be fitted with an anti-mine system, to locate and identify limpets and dispose of them as divers are expected to at present. A vehicle can maintain a twenty-four hour watch; it would take a considerable number of divers to do the same.

The vehicle would be powerful, but as compact as possible, and fitted with the lightest umbilical available. All parts of the vehicle would be modular, to enhance maintenance. Technical electronic and weapons pods could be added to keep in line with future developments and operational requirements. Because of the vehicle's make up, it would be a viable production model, and could be financially justified. Could tomorrow's combat frogman be replaced by a machine?

Bibliography

A. Cecil Hampshire, *The Secret Navies* (William Kimber, London).

Philip Warner, *The Special Air Service* (William Kimber, London).

James D. Ladd, *The Special Boat Squadron* (Arms and Armour Press, London).

Derek Boyd, *The Royal Engineer* (Leo Cooper Ltd, London).

The Royal Engineer Journal (Royal Engineers, Royal School of Military Engineering).

T.J. Waldrom and James Gleeson, *The Frogman* (The Elmfield Press).

R.H. Davis, *Deep Diving and Submarine Operations* (The Saint Catherine Press Ltd.)

James D. Ladd, *The Royal Marines 1919–1980* (Arms and Armour Press, London).

Tony Geraghty, *Who Dares Wins* (Arms and Armour Press).

Tony Geraghty, *This is the SAS* (Arms and Armour Press).

The Royal Navy Diving Manual.

The United States Navy Diving Manual.

Soldier of Fortune Magazine.

Forrest G. Wood, *Marine Mammals and Man: The Navy's Porpoises and Sea Lions* (Robert B. Luce Inc, Washington).

Index

Subskimmer moves at high speed.